YORK UNIVERSITY
Invitation Lecture Series
1964

RELIGION AND THE UNIVERSITY

THE FRANK GERSTEIN LECTURES

January and February 1964

Religion

AND THE

University

JAROSLAV JAN PELIKAN
WILLIAM G. POLLARD
CHARLES MOELLER
MAURICE N. EISENDRATH
ALEXANDER WITTENBERG

Published *for* YORK UNIVERSITY *by*
UNIVERSITY OF TORONTO PRESS

The Publishers wish to thank Literary Master-
works, Inc., and Philosophical Library, Inc., for
permission to reproduce excerpts from *What Is
Literature?* by J.-P. Sartre; City Lights Books for
permission to quote from the poem *"Howl"* from
Howl and Other Poems by Allen Ginsberg;
Duquesne University Press for permission to quote
from *Truth and Freedom* by L. de Raeymaeker,
et al.; Curtis, Brown Ltd., and *Harper's Magazine*
for permission to quote from "The College Scene"
by Michael Novak.

Introduction

THE papers reproduced in the pages that follow were, with one exception, presented during the 1964 winter term at York University. They constitute the Gerstein Lectures, the third in a series of Invitation Lectures delivered at the University and generously supported by a grant from the Frank Gerstein Foundation. Following the lectures, and as a result of the very considerable interest aroused by the lectures, a panel discussion–seminar of faculty and students was held to permit further consideration of the topic. At this meeting Professor Alexander Wittenberg expressed a view somewhat different than that put forward by any of the lecturers. He was asked to incorporate these ideas in a paper, a request to which he was good enough to accede, and we are happy to include his paper in this book.

The fact that "Religion and the University," the theme selected for the 1964 series, occasioned some surprise, if not consternation, in the University is a matter which, in itself, is of considerable interest. There are some who assume that because a university by its very nature must consistently raise questions and search out new truths, it cannot deal with religion in which, it is suggested, truth is already presumed to be known. There are others who assume that, because of the traditional separation of Church and State, any state supported institution must scrupulously avoid any discussion of religion. Both of these assumptions are, I believe, false.

It is not my place to discuss this matter in any detail—this will be done more effectively in the chapters that follow—but let me at least suggest why I think these assumptions are erroneous and why we selected "Religion and the University" as the theme of the 1964 lecture series.

First, as my colleague Professor Wittenberg has said, religion is part of social reality and cannot be ignored by any university which seeks to understand man and civilization. Can history, for example, be taught without reference to religion and its impact on the development of ideas and ideals in every nation in the world and in every period of history? Can sociology be taught without some understanding of the institutionalization of religion and of its influence on the customs and mores of any given community or society? Can psychology be taught without some understanding of religion as a force which influences, regulates, and even directs the behaviour of many individuals? Surely the answers to such questions must be in the negative. Indeed, religion is discussed in many courses, such as Professor William Kilbourn's course in Humanities at this University; religion is the subject of considerable research by outstanding social scientists such as Professor Gordon Allport, whose work focuses on the relation of religious beliefs and every day behaviour; and religion has a recurrent place in the content of every comprehensive and authoritative book in the social and behavioural sciences. And what is true of the few disciplines I have mentioned is also true of other disciplines, including English and philosophy. The fact is that religion *is* part of objective reality and cannot honesty be excluded from the curriculum of a university.

The argument that any university—private or state-supported—can ignore religion, is quite unrealistic. There can be no question that religion must have consideration in a vital university. There are, however, some important and highly relevant questions which can be raised in any discussion of "Religion and the University." The first must relate to the manner in which religion is considered by the various disciplines in a university. Must religion be subjected to the same cold analysis to which the scientist subjects natural phenomena, or would this approach actually prevent an understanding of religion because faith and belief are such essential ingredients? Does the scientific approach to the study of religion actually permit full comprehension of religion? If not, is any other method of study tolerable in a university?

A different and more difficult question is whether there is a place in a university, and in a state university particularly, for a department or faculty, or school, devoted exclusively to the study of religion? Can a university, without developing a partisan or denominational approach, develop a faculty in which there is a general and genuine interest in the study of religion and the religions of man?

A third question one must ask relates to the place of religion in the informal or extracurricular programme of a university. Is there a place for religious services in such a programme? For the discussion of religious problems? For a university chaplain? For a university chapel? Here many people are adamant, for even if they agree that religion is a legitimate subject for critical study in a university they vehemently resist the idea of religion being used as a proselytizing force on the campus. Others argue that help is provided for students to organize athletic teams, debating clubs, political organizations, art clubs, and, therefore, similar help should be provided to those students who wish to study or worship together.

There are other issues, of course, which will arise in the chapters that follow, but the above were the compelling reasons and issues that led us at York University to plan a lecture series around the topic "Religion and the University." I hope all who read this volume will find that the effort was justified and that fresh light is thrown on an extremely complex and difficult problem.

The production of this book owes much to Mr. Timothy E. Reid who carried much of the burden not only of organizing the lectures, but also of collecting and editing the manuscripts and working out the many details of publication.

MURRAY G. ROSS,
President

Contents

In Defence of Research
in Religious Studies
at the Secular University

Jaroslav Jan Pelikan

Jaroslav Jan Pelikan

Jaroslav Jan Pelikan is the Titus Street Professor of Ecclesiastical History, Yale University. Following his graduation from Concordia College, Fort Wayne, Indiana, in 1942, Dr. Pelikan completed his studies at the University of Chicago. A minister of the Lutheran Church, he has taught at several universities in the United States and in 1963–64 was Director of Graduate Studies, Department of Religious Studies, Yale University. Among his writings are: The Shape of Death, The Light of the World, *and* The Riddle of Roman Catholicism. *Dr. Pelikan is editor and translator of thirteen volumes of* Luther's Works.

R ELIGION, to paraphrase Clemenceau's famous remark
about war, is too important a part of life and culture
to be left only to the clergy. Likewise, research in religion
is too important a part of scholarly inquiry to be left only to
the theologians. Such research therefore forms an essential
part of the work of the secular university. In those cultures
and periods of history in which the Church has created,
nourished, and controlled the university, it could, of course,
be assumed that such research was a legitimate part of the
university's task. Harvard was established because the
founders dreaded "to leave an illiterate ministry to the
churches, when our present ministers shall lie in the dust,"
and Yale was established because it was feared that Harvard was being unfaithful to this religious charter. The
history of higher education in this Dominion, and especially
in this Province, has been shaped by the same assumption.
In fact, most of the private colleges and universities in
North America, and several of the public institutions as
well, owe their origin to religious foundations which regarded religious studies as essential to the university's curriculum and research in religion as basic to its programme
of scholarship and publication.

That assumption can no longer be taken for granted in
the academic community. During the nineteenth century,
when the title "university" came into general use (Toronto
in 1827, Yale in 1887, etc.), the warrant for the inclusion
of research in religion at the secular university came under
increasingly critical examination. Two of the most noted
discussions of the question were prepared by professors at
the University of Berlin more than a hundred years apart,
Friedrich Schleiermacher and Adolf Harnack.[1] Each of
them was the dominant figure in the German Protestant

[1]Friedrich Schleiermacher, "Gelegentliche Gedanken über Universitä-
ten in deutschem Sinn" (1808) in Theodor Schulz and Erich Weniger
(eds.), *Pädagogische Schriften*, II (Düsseldorf, 1957), 81–139; Adolf
Harnack, "Die Bedeutung der theologischen Fakultäten" in *Erforschtes
und Erlebtes* (Giessen, 1923), pp. 199–217; also Adolf Harnack, "Die

theology of his day, and each sought to defend, in his own highly characteristic fashion, the place of the Christian, specifically Protestant, theological faculty in the university. Despite such eminent advocacy, the propriety of research in religious studies at the university continues to be a matter of controversy and discussion on both sides of the Atlantic and on both sides of the border which your country shares with mine.

The juxtaposition of Schleiermacher and Harnack in this great debate is all the more interesting because of the contrast between the distinctive emphases for which they are known in the history of Christian thought. Schleiermacher, more perhaps even than Kierkegaard, is the apostle of religious subjectivity, of the primacy of experience, indeed of *Gefühl*, in religion, over against any effort to objectify it in a set of dogma, in ritual, or in an institution.[2] Harnack, on the other hand, is still spoken of in awe as the high priest of objective historical research, who could assert the right of research in religion to be taken seriously simply by pointing to his own achievements as a scholar, author, and editor.[3] Both Schleiermacher and Harnack, therefore, recognized the centrality of the issue of scholarly objectivity in any consideration of the right of research in religion to belong to the community of scholarship. As the natural sciences, the humanities, and the social sciences have grown increasingly sophisticated about methodology, defenders of that right have become increasingly defensive, and perforce increasingly modest, about the methods of research proper to research in religious studies.

Aufgabe der theologischen Fakultäten und die allgemeine Religionsgeschichte, nebst einem Nachwort" (1901) in *Reden und Aufsätze*, II (Giessen, 1904), 161–187.

[2]Cf. Jaroslav Pelikan, "The Vocation of the Christian Apologist: A Study of Schleiermacher's *Reden*" in Edwin H. Rian (ed.), *Christianity and World Revolution* (New York, 1963), pp. 173–89.

[3]Cf. Jaroslav Pelikan, "Introduction" to Adolf Harnack, *The Mission and Expansion of Christianity in the First Three Centuries*, tr. James Moffatt (Torchbook edition; New York, 1961).

Even in the universities that continue to carry on such research, there are many professors in other fields who have grave misgivings about the academic propriety and intellectual respectability of this research. And alas, the quality and scholarly standards set for this research by some of its devotees seem determined to do everything possible to confirm these misgivings. In the area of religious studies seminars are sometimes offered and dissertations accepted that would be drummed out of the regiment in other parts of the university; and the pietist and the secularist, in a strange alliance, will regard this as quite proper, being agreed that faith and learning should be separate. But even research of unquestionable excellence is obliged today to explain why it still belongs in the secular university. Most of the objections to it can be summarized under two questions: Can research in religious studies be sufficiently scholarly and objective to warrant certification by the university? And can it be sufficiently disengaged from both the evangelistic and the professional concerns to be a scholarly field among scholarly fields? These are not, I am sure, merely two forms of the same question. But in this lecture I propose to deal with them in order, for only when the question of scholarly objectivity has been faced can the implications of research in religion both for the religious life of the university community and for the training of the clergy be addressed.

"To write the history of a religion," wrote Ernest Renan in his *Vie de Jésus* just over a hundred years ago, "it is necessary, first, to have believed it (otherwise we should not be able to understand how it has charmed and satisfied the human conscience); in the second place, to believe it no longer in an absolute manner, for absolute faith is incompatible with sincere history."[4] And that, as the *New Yorker* would say, is the neatest trick of the week! For one thing, Renan does not specify what mixture of fond memory and

[4]Ernest Renan, *Life of Jesus* (English translation; New York, 1927), p. 65.

cool scepticism is the proper one for the achievement of the
desired balance, or whether the mixture remains the same
for an interpreter of, let us say, Montanism and Roman
Catholicism—entirely apart from the question of how one
can "have believed" a religious system which has had no
adherents for a millennium or more! For that matter, the
research that Renan himself carried on does not exemplify
any such satisfying balance, unless romantic wistfulness be
termed an adequate substitute for commitment and positi-
vism be equated with scholarship. Nevertheless, Renan's
methodological prescription does raise the problem of
scholarly objectivity in a piquant way, and thus may serve
as a text for our examination of the problem of objectivity.

I

Forgive me if I begin with a *tu quoque* argument. The
attack upon research in religious studies had much of its
origin in the hey-day of scientism, when it was assumed
that because the natural sciences are based upon accurate
measurement and upon laboratory experiments that can be
verified through repetition, they lead to hypotheses that
gradually become conclusions as the evidence accumulates.
Thus the methodology of the natural sciences was thought
to be objective throughout, because their very principles
and procedures screened out the subjectivity of the experi-
menter and observer. Coinciding as it did with the golden
age of historical research in the nineteenth century and
with the beginnings of the study of human personality and
society towards the end of that century, this dedication to
the scientific method had a decisive effect upon the presuppositions of these disciplines as well.[5] Leopold von Ranke's
famous dictum about describing history *wie es eigentlich*

---

[5]See the comments of Benedetto Croce, *History: Its Theory and
Practice*, tr. Douglas Ainslie (New York, 1960), pp. 292ff.

gewesen has undoubtedly been caricatured by critics who
were not worthy to unloose the latchet of his historical
shoes—much less to fill the shoes! Yet it does bespeak a
naïveté about the interaction between the intellect, the will,
and the emotions as this affects a man's apprehension and
interpretation of facts past or present.[6] The beginnings of
the social sciences were equally presumptuous about their
objectivity, and perhaps with even less justification.

In the name of the objectivity of the scientific method,
research in religious study was denounced as dogmatism, as
indoctrination, as the extension of inner feelings and therefore the pursuit of a will-o'-the-wisp which was, by definition,
unverifiable. The notorious disagreements of theologians
over the correct interpretation of texts in the Bible
became proof that an exegete finds in Scripture whatever
meaning he wants to find and that there is no external curb
upon this caprice. Similarly, the quarrels—for example,
between the authors of the Magdeburg *Centuries* and
Caesar Baronius[7]—over the *testimonia patrum* and the use
of Christian antiquities as a weapon in interconfessional
polemics seemed to show that church history is different
from other history in degree if not actually in kind, simply
because the church historian has such a stake in the out-
come of his researches. (It should probably be added that
Protestant church historians have been as ready to apply
this criticism to their Roman Catholic colleagues as have
secular historians to regard it as a characteristic of all
church history.[8]) Because research in religion thus was
lacking in objective verifiability and because there were as

[6]G. P. Gooch, *History and Historians in the Nineteenth Century*
(2nd ed.; Boston, 1959), pp. 72–121.
[7]Cf. Ferdinand Christian Baur, *Die Epochen der kirchlichen Ge-
schichtsschreibung* (1852) (Hildesheim, 1962), pp. 39–107; Harry Elmer
Barnes, *A History of Historical Writing* (2nd ed.; New York, 1962),
pp. 121–35.
[8]See the fine summary by Wilhelm Pauck, "The Roman Catholic
Critique of Protestantism," *The Heritage of the Reformation* (2nd ed.;
Glencoe, Ill., 1961), pp. 231ff.

many opinions as there were teachers, it could not claim to belong in the community of scholarly inquiry, but could be relegated to the area of private judgment and personal taste.

During the past generation this situation has been drastically revised—not because of a sudden upsurge of piety among secular historians, but because of a growing recognition that there is no such thing as an uninterpreted fact and that therefore an exegesis free of presuppositions is impossible, not only for the student of Isaiah but also for the researcher into fossils or the historian of Latin literature. As a result of the work of Collingwood, Croce, and many other historians and philosophers, including the late Charles Norris Cochrane of Toronto,[9] everyone today agrees that the problem of objectivity and presupposition is not peculiar to the field of religion; nor is it, at least in the modern world, most vexing there. The criticisms I have been reciting have combined with the history of critical thought within the religious traditions to make the student of religious history and phenomena acutely aware of the question. Consequently, the chief difference between the colleagues I have had as a member of various departments of history over the years and the colleagues I have known as a member of departments and faculties of religion is that the students of religious ideas and institutions are both more aware and more explicit about their "position" than are many of their historical colleagues. The most basic problem is not the presence of presuppositions that may colour one's judgment; it is the awareness of these presuppositions, the ability to deal with them methodologically, and the effect they may have on one's capacity to pick up the signals of an alien system or doctrine. Some sets of presuppositions—for example, certain species of contemporary

[9]R. G. Collingwood, *The Idea of History* (New York, 1956); Croce, *History: Its Theory and Practice*; C. N. Cochrane, *Thucydidies and the Science of History* (London, 1929); Wilhelm Dilthey, *Pattern and Meaning in History*, ed. H. P. Rickman (New York, 1962).

existentialism—may shut one off so completely from anything external or past or foreign that one has virtually no antenna left. The presence of such presuppositions would constitute a valid ground for objection to a scholar, not because of the correctness or incorrectness of the theological position itself but because of its effect on his capacity for research. But this would be true of other disciplines as well as of religious studies.

II

It is essential to keep in mind, when we are speaking about research in religious studies, that such research includes a range of interests and scholarly areas across a large part of the humanities. Perhaps the most nearly analogous situation is that of a department of history, where an Egyptologist and a student of international relations since World War II are both called historians. Of course, with increasing specialization and its counterpart, the cross-fertilization of disciplines which is so dear to the heart of present-day educational theorists, such a range is beginning to characterize most of the departments in the university, with a consequent breakdown of communication within the disciplines that used to take place only between the disciplines. Departments are now clusters of sub-departments, each with its own data and methods. And, as I do not need to remind the new president of a new university, it vastly complicates the procedure of appointment and promotion when one physicist cannot assess the work of another because their specialities are so far apart. Yet the sheer weight of age and tradition forces the study of religion into an acceptance of such a pluralism of fields and tasks.

This pluralism has special relevance for the problem of scholarly objectivity. Both the case for objectivity and the very definition of it will be different in the different subfields of religious studies. There are certainly some areas of research in religious studies upon whose scientific chastity no other scholar, or at least no other humanist, would cast any aspersions. Perhaps the best illustration is the textual criticism of the New Testament, in relation to the methods of textual criticism as applied to other bodies of literature. From its beginnings in the work of the humanists, especially Erasmus, the textual criticism of the New Testament has developed in close conjunction with classical scholarship.[10] Indeed, many of the methods and principles we now apply to determine the best possible reading—as I do, for example, in my own work as an editor of the works of Martin Luther—originated with the textual critics of the New Testament. In the eighteenth century Johann Albrecht Bengel set down the principle that *lectio difficilior praeferenda est*, that is, that in a conflict between two equally attested readings we should prefer the one that is harder to explain, because a later transcriber would be more likely to simplify the text with the thought of correcting it than to complicate it.[11] This principle, when applied with imagination and discernment, is still valid, both in the study of the Bible and in humanistic scholarship generally. And a student of Elizabethan literature whose own scholarly career depends upon the work of the textual critic of the First Folio with variations is obligated to accord a place in the charmed circle of scholarship to the textual criticism of the New Testament, whose critical apparatus makes the *Variorum Shakespeare* look like a verbatim transcript.

The trouble is that although the textual criticism of the New Testament deals with a religious text, it seems to be

[10]In general, see Vincent A. Dearing, *A Manual of Textual Analysis* (Berkeley, 1959); Marvin R. Vincent, *A History of the Textual Criticism of the New Testament* (New York, 1899).

[11]Cf. John Christian Burk, *A Memoir of the Life and Writings of John Albrecht Bengel*, tr. Robert Francis Walker (London, 1842), pp. 224–50; Jaroslav Pelikan, "In Memoriam Johann Albrecht Bengel, June 24, 1687 to November 2, 1752," *Concordia Theological Monthly*, XXIII (1952), 785–96.

one of the least religious fields in religious studies. Thus one could measure objectivity and scholarly acceptability with a filter that permits only the violet and ultra-violet rays to pass, namely, those that are coolest, but that screens out the red end of the spectrum as too warm. Research in religious studies would then be justified to the extent that it foreswore its interest in religion. For there are areas of religious study and ways of working in them that are so wrapped up in normative judgments that no one in the public realm can evaluate them. I am thinking, for example, of fields like dogmatic and moral theology. These are the truly troublesome areas, for they are also the ones that are most explicitly "religious" or at least the most churchly. Eliminating these areas *a priori* would be a Draconian solution to the problem of objectivity and would run the danger of trivializing research in religious studies by permitting it to do only those tasks about whose scholarly results no one inside or outside the churches will be disturbed.

Do such studies as moral and dogmatic theology deserve the name "research" as this name is understood by the university? It seems to me that they do, or more accurately, that they can, provided that there is in them a major component of scholarship that can be validated according to publicly verifiable procedures of disciplined study. Dogmatic theology, for example, has usually been shaped by biblical, historical, or philosophical study, or by some combination of two or of all three of these. Which of the three ought to play which role in dogmatic theology is a matter of much controversy among the theologians and between the churches, but each of the three components is a humanistic discipline whose materials and methods are accessible to any scholar with the necessary technical and linguistic equipment. On the basis of this criterion, there are some kinds of Christian dogmatics that would qualify as legitimate areas of research, and some kinds that would not. (Most of those that would not, to be honest, are those that

would not want to and would, in fact, glory in their very
exclusion.) For that matter, some ways of doing biblical
exegesis would pass muster, while others would not; and
even some methods of church history would certainly be
ruled out. It so happens that I—speaking now as a church-
man and theologian rather than as a university professor—
believe that this same criterion applies to any teaching and
writing in religious studies, whether in the secular university
or in a school directly under the Church. But the university
has its own reasons for insisting on this criterion, and I
think that the reasons are sound.

III

The case for research in religious studies at the secular
university is part of the case for general education and for
its bearing upon all education, including and especially
graduate education. I must confess that I am speaking here
in ignorance of the present state of your thought at York
University about general education and its relation to both
specialized and professional study. Perhaps this ignorance
is an asset, at least temporarily, for it will permit me to
develop my case without knowing ahead of time whose pet
cause I am espousing or criticizing. As one who took his
doctorate at the University of Chicago in the years of
Robert Maynard Hutchins and who became a professor at
Yale in the years of A. Whitney Griswold, I could perhaps
be expected to have a strong prejudice in favour of what a
recent book has called "the poor old liberal arts," and I
have. This is not so much because of either President
Hutchins or President Griswold, to both of whom I owe
much, as because of my own work as a scholar and teacher
who has discovered that the secret component or *x*-factor
in truly significant research, at least in my field, is frequently the factor that could not have been supplied by any

number of hours of further digging in the sources, but only by a close and continuing acquaintance with the best in our entire heritage of thought and literature.

Such a prejudice in favour of general education becomes most evident at the level of undergraduate education, in what most Canadian universities still call "arts." But as a graduate professor I am concerned with the implications of general education for research and graduate teaching, and I would argue that the presence of presuppositions in the work of the scholar or graduate student is an advantage rather than a disadvantage, because it is one of the most effective ways of relating the specialization of the scholar to the general issues of education, and indeed of humanity, with which he is obliged to deal. There is probably no field more distant from my own expertise than the field of cybernetics, the study of analogies between the ways of human thought and the functioning of mechanical systems of communication and computation. But I am impressed by the capacity of the human mind to transcend itself and to reflect on its own processes—even on their analogy to computers. This capacity for self-transcendence is the instrument that creates an awareness of hidden assumptions in scholarship. When Anders Nygren speaks of "the role of the self-evident in history," he is referring to those concepts and convictions about which a writer does not speak because he does not have to, but into which the historian must seek to penetrate because he cannot understand what the author says unless he grasps also what the author means without saying it.[12] It is to these self-evident axioms of our own thought and work that we are driven when the question of objectivity and presupposition compels us to reflect on our own discipline and its hidden assumptions.

When we thus face the challenge of presuppositions squarely, we are enabled to come at general education, not

[12]Anders Nygren, "The Role of the Self-Evident in History," *Journal of Religion*, XXVIII (1948), 235–41.

before our specialization or around it, but through it. There are philosophers who argue that the scholar must clarify his presuppositions before he begins his research, for otherwise his research will be lacking in intellectual integrity. No one can paralyze an academic discussion more quickly than one of these bright but brittle colleagues who scoffs at "mere erudition" and insists that every game be played according to his ground rules, which seemingly permit one, by a judicious manipulation of the meaning of meaning and the nature of verification, to speak about any discipline, whether he knows anything about it or not.

> The heathen in his blindness
> From Sydney to Cadiz,
> Is always talking nonsense
> And doesn't know he is.
> Then let us spread the glorious news,
> Whose truth is undeniable,
> That nothing has significance
> But what is verifiable.[13]

It seems to me that the process of self-examination is more fruitful when one has acquired a self to examine, and that this is as true of academic disciplines as it is of human personalities.

When we sound the depths of our own disciplines and begin to see what binds them to others and what makes them distinctive, we simultaneously address the question of general education and refine our own disciplines. Any university that attempts to undertake this assignment without paying attention to religious studies is cutting itself off from one of the richest resources available to it for this very quest. The scholarly subject-matter of religious studies is inevitably broader than its administrative province in any

[13]E. L. Mascall, "A Hymn for Logical Empiricists," *Pi in the High* (London, 1959), p. 12.

modern university. One thinks, for example, of the virtual
monopoly which anthropologists and social psychologists
have acquired in the area of primitive religion, or of the
dominance of political and literary historians in the field of
Puritan studies from Professor Woodhouse of this city to
the late lamented Perry Miller. Throughout the humanities,
then, there are scholars dealing with data that would be a
proper subject for research in religious studies, and this is
as it should be. But this distribution of research in religious
studies does provide a setting for a university-wide consideration of the presuppositions of general education, in which
research in religious studies may render a service to the rest
of the university precisely because of its self-consciousness
about the relation between fact and interpretation. Research
in religious studies must, in turn, be informed and called to
account by such an exchange with the methods and materials of its sister disciplines, as indeed it has been over and
over again.

IV

Within the context of these observations on the problem of
objectivity in research on religion, we may now consider
the bearing of such research on two related aspects of religion at the university: the training of the clergy and the
personal commitment of the student. I am, of course, aware
that York University does not now, and probably never
will, include expressly theological colleges in its administrative structure, leaving the nuances of mediating between
such colleges to its older sister institution. Nevertheless, the
case I have been trying to make does not hold unless it can
be applied specifically to ministerial education as well. In
addition, it will be inevitable that the research and graduate
study carried out at this university will draw students who
will work in the churches and seminaries; therefore we

cannot ignore the implications of research in religious studies for theological study.

At least since Peter Abailard led a mass emigration of students at Paris, the study of theology by the present and future servants of the Church has sought a structure for its work and a definition for its task that would keep it related responsibly to the empirical Church without involving it in the domestic quarrels of clergy, bishops, and people. The reorganization of the Continental and British universities during the Renaissance and Reformation accorded an honoured and secure place to professors of divinity;[14] and if we are to judge by the scholarly fruits, the habilitation of research in religious studies within the university has unquestionably been a blessing for the disciplined study of theology and thus for the education of the clergy. But it has not been an unmixed blessing. In the eighteenth century, the Evangelical Revival in Great Britain and Pietism on the Continent were agreed that academic theology had been so alienated from the Church that the professors of divinity at the universities were not fit to teach the preachers of the Gospel.[15] Shaped as they were by this mood of evangelicalism and Pietism, many of the Protestants who came to Canada and the United States were determined that their ministers would be trained in an atmosphere where true piety and sound learning were properly mixed. As a result, most of the Protestant clergy in both our countries are educated in schools that are directly responsible to the boards of some denomination.[16] Even a scholar like myself,

[14]Cf. Charles Augustus Briggs, *History of the Study of Theology* (New York, 1916), II, 82–142, on Renaissance and Reformation.

[15]Sidney E. Mead, "The Rise of the Evangelical Conception of the Ministry in America 1607–1850" in H. Richard Niebuhr and Daniel Day Williams (eds.), *The Ministry in Historical Perspectives* (New York, 1956), pp. 207–49.

[16]H. Richard Niebuhr, Daniel Day Williams, and James M. Gustafson, *The Advancement of Theological Education* (New York, 1957), pp. 1–26.

who is not now involved in such a school and who owes most of his own scholarship to the inspiration of German *Universitätstheologie*, must acknowledge that our system has been successful.

Yet it has often been impoverished because of its exclusive preoccupation within the Church at the expense of the university. The education of the clergy needs to be tied to the churches, but it also needs to feel the tug at its sleeve that only the free university can supply. In support let me cite the authority of Martin Luther, as he explains what made him a Reformer: "I never wanted to do it, and I do not want to do it now. I was forced and driven into this position in the first place when I became a Doctor of Theology. As a Doctor in a general free university, I began . . . to do what such a Doctor is sworn to do, expounding the Scriptures for all the world and teaching everybody. Once in this position, I have had to stay in it, and I cannot give it up or leave it with a good conscience. . . . For what I began as a Doctor . . . I must truly confess to the end of my life."[17] Luther's position as a Doctor of Theology in the university bound him to the Church, yet it gave him the freedom he needed to serve the Church as an obedient rebel —to quote the title of my forthcoming book on "Catholic substance and Protestant principle in Luther's Reformation." What the American and Canadian churches continue to need is to have at least some of the research in religious studies carried on by those who are, as Luther was, "Doctors in a general free university"—willing to act responsibly, able to act freely. Only such research will be able to do for the churches what the churches need but often cannot or will not do for themselves. And only as a result of such research will the ministers of those churches receive an education instead of merely a training.

[17]Cf. Jaroslav Pelikan, *Luther the Expositor* (Saint Louis, 1959), pp. 46–47.

V

Even in this discussion of theological education I have not dealt with the problem of the commitments of the individual student or the relevance of the sort of research I have been describing for those commitments. The case for research and study in religion at the secular university is sometimes based on the claim that the religious life and the commitment of the student are inevitably enhanced by such research. I must confess that I cannot share this simple-minded optimism, for both my historical study and my personal experience as a student and teacher have shown me that the implications of research in religious studies for personal commitment are extremely tenuous, and that the personal effects of such research in the student's life of faith and obedience can be exceedingly ambiguous. A recent research project by Father Greeley provides statistical support for the view that there is no one-to-one relation between academic study and personal religion.[18]

Over the past twenty years I have known some graduate students—and not merely members of snake-handling cults—who have lost their religious faith completely and (so it seems) permanently in the course of their research in religious studies. I have known others who only through such research have discovered the vitality of the Judaeo-Christian tradition, which they had long given up for dead, and who thus found their way back to the faith of their fathers. I have known yet others who came to such research with very little personal faith, who in their research examined what they had as well as what others, past and present, had, and who went on their way from such research with just about as little as they had brought, albeit in a somewhat more chaste and disciplined form. As a Christian believer

18Andrew M. Greeley, *Religion and Career: A Study of College Graduates* (New York, 1963).

and as an orthodox theologian, I care about this process deeply, and seek as an ordained servant of the Church to apply the healing power of Word and Sacrament to those who are engaged in this struggle. But finally this is not our doing, nor should it be. The issue of such struggles lies with the grace of One who is not the captive of our research.

But as a scholar and a professor in a general free university, I must view this process with the very objectivity I seek to apply to my own research. In my own field of the history of Christian thought, I am, as a Christian, pleased if a student, through his research or perhaps even through mine, receives the grace to decide to take up residence in the household of faith, if he learns to eat at its banquet table and to die in its family circle. But as a historian whose research in religious studies has taken him through the labyrinthine ways of the Church's history, all I can require of such a student is that he give me an accurate description of the furniture. And as a whole person, both scholar and believer, I am willing to say that any religious faith ought to be able and willing to take its chances on this process, or it will not be worthy either of our scholarly research or of our personal commitment.

The Recovery
of Theological Perspective
in a Scientific Age

William G. Pollard

William G. Pollard

*William G. Pollard is Executive Director, Oak Ridge Insti-
tute of Nuclear Studies, a non-profit corporation of thirty-
nine southern universities in the United States which
conducts programmes under contract primarily for the
Atomic Energy Commission. Dr. Pollard received his doctorate in theoretical physics at Rice University. Since being
ordained in 1954, he has served as Priest Associate in St.
Stephen's Episcopal Church in Oak Ridge, Tennessee. Dr.
Pollard has written and lectured on many subjects.* Physicist
and Christian *and* Chance and Providence *are perhaps the
widest known of his works.*

THE second half of the twentieth century will certainly go down in history as the golden age of science. That movement of the human imagination and spirit called science, which came into being in seventeenth-century Europe, has grown with infectious power among us during the intervening three centuries. Only in this century, however, has it come to full flower, and not until the end of World War II did men generally speak naturally of "The Scientific Age." The immense and sparkling achievements of science command our attention on every side. The spirit of the age dominates every educational force which influences each of us from infancy to maturity, and typically scientific styles of thought are imposed upon us in every area of inquiry.

In the midst of such an age, theology finds itself in grave difficulties. The Judaeo-Christian, biblical type of thought, which for so many centuries governed the whole outlook of Western man, is alien to the contemporary scientific style. Theologians today struggle and suffer with this sense of alienation, and there is much discussion about making the Gospel "relevant" to modern man. One of the leading figures in this movement is Rudolf Bultmann with his programme of extricating the Christian message from its first-century context by removing from it what, under the canons of modern thought, must be regarded as mythological elements. Another approach is that of Dietrich Bonhoeffer with his call for a "non-religious" theology or that of Paul Tillich with his replacement of God as transcendent being with an ontological "ground of being."

Quite recently the Bishop of Woolwich in his widely read little book, *Honest to God*, has given fresh emphasis to this problem. Although reflecting primarily the thought of Bultmann, Bonhoeffer, and Tillich, the honesty and simplicity of Dr. Robinson's way of expressing his difficulties have given his book a popular appeal far beyond that of the theologians on which he depends. For many non-theological readers within and without the Church he has struck a sympathetic and responsive note, because the problems which trouble him are certainly genuine and well-nigh universal in the contemporary world.

It is in this context that I wish to discuss the topic of this series, "Religion and the University." More than any other institution of society, the university maintains and nourishes the spirit of the age. If domination of the oncoming generation by typically scientific styles of thought is to be relieved somewhat, and recovery of the strength and power of the Judaeo-Christian heritage of Western man begun, it is the university which must do it. My thesis is that modern man has lost a capacity to respond to and to know a whole range of reality external to himself which Western man in earlier centuries quite naturally possessed. My purpose is to challenge the university to seek actively recovery of this lost capacity. Thus the title of my lecture is "The Recovery of Theological Perspective in a Scientific Age."

Every age is the victim of its own style of thought. One does not generally see this about his own age, but in the retrospect of history, when the style of thought has changed radically, one can see it about past ages. In recounting the history of the rise of science, it is common to express amazement at the blindness of mediaeval scholastic thought. Many questions which the schoolmen attempted to answer by appeals to authority could easily have been settled empirically. It is astounding to us that it never seemed to occur to anyone then simply to observe how things actually were, or to make simple experimental tests of their conclusions. In retrospect we can see clearly, as they could not, how inescapably imprisoned they were in their particular system and style of thought. Moreover, it was a slow and painstaking process to liberate Western man from this intellectual prison, as the history of science in the sixteenth and seventeenth centuries shows. Yet this fact should cause us to reflect on the nature of the imprisonment which our own style of thought has placed upon us.

The transformation from the mediaeval to the scientific world view has led to revolutionary changes in our apprehension of the natural order and a profound enrichment in our understanding of the inner harmony of the structures which undergird nature. These are the direct scientific achievements of this transformation and they are all good. But the transformation has also been accompanied by more subtle secondary changes in our whole mode and style of thought about reality. These changes have come about largely unconsciously as a result of the vigour and inner dynamism of the scientific enterprise, its breathtaking pace, and brilliant achievements. Few today realize how restrictive and binding our contemporary style of thought really is. It excludes whole segments of external reality from our apprehension and understanding. It also severely limits the kinds of questions which can be meaningfully addressed to any given sequence of events in time. It is a style of thought and set of criteria for admissible questions which are admirably suited to the scientific enterprise. But it is at the same time a style of thought which drastically limits the possibility of thinking biblically about reality.

Alfred North Whitehead in his book, *Science and the Modern World*, comments that "every philosophy is tinged with the colouring of some secret imaginative background, which never emerges explicitly into its trains of reasoning." What are the characteristics of our contemporary style of thought? What is the particular secret imaginative background which colours our efforts to experience and to know reality? First, the contemporary style consistently avoids all reference to reality transcendent to space and time. Science is by definition the study of nature. By nature we mean the sum total of objects and events in three-dimensional space and time. It is the mission of science to go as far as it can in understanding all objects and events in space and time in terms of other objects and events in space and time. Any mode of understanding in which any aspect of nature depends on something transcendent to nature is not scientific understanding. Science as such does not reject such modes of understanding; it simply ignores them. It cannot do anything else and still be science. This produces a style of thought in which the transcendent and the supernatural simply never appear.

Science for all its wonderful achievements has been steadily leading our culture into an ever increasing bondage to that portion of reality which we call nature. Each generation during the rise of science has had less capacity than the last to respond to and maintain an awareness of reality transcendent to nature, and each has at the same time taken us further on a journey into the intellectual and spiritual prison of our present bondage to space, time, and matter. For all their scientific brilliance, they have been years of gathering darkness as the real and substantial existence of the supernatural order has slowly faded and disappeared. Modern man has become a complete solipsist with respect to the whole range of mankind's traditional and age-old experience of the invisible and unseen world transcendent to nature. As the vast reaches of space, measured in billions of light-years, have been opened through science to man's apprehension, the domain of reality within which space is immersed and which everywhere interpenetrates it, as would other dimensions perpendicular to it, has correspondingly shrunk to nothing. There is no place left for heaven, and modern man cannot even conceive of any way of getting out of space or of any reality not contained within it. In like manner as the vast ranges of time, measured in billions of years, have been made understandable to man, so much the more has the dimension of eternity perpendicular to time faded from our apprehension.

As far back into the roots of human experience as archaeology has been able to take us, man's apprehension of the unseen world of supernatural reality has been as lively and vivid as that of the seen world of nature. In art and literature, in music and poetry, in liturgy and worship, among all races and cultures from the primitive to the most advanced, we find the evidence of this central fact of human experience. Indeed, the function of the arts and poetry has always been to provide the means by which men could share and communicate with each other their experience of the supernatural, in the same way that mathematics and conceptual language are the proper means for sharing and communicating our experience of nature. Yet art predates language as a medium of communication among early cultures and was developed naturally and independently among all those of which any appreciable trace has been preserved. Throughout the whole wide range and diversity of human experience, with the sole exception of the West in the nineteenth and twentieth centuries, the world of nature has been alive with, and immersed within, a supernatural world which everywhere made contact with it, although was transcendent to it. It is this whole dimension of reality which the scientific age has lost the capacity to experience or know.

An age such as ours which has lost a genuine capacity for knowing and responding to some great segment of reality is actually, without knowing it, in a dark age. There is, of course, so much sparkle and achievement in present-day science that it seems incredible to speak of the twentieth century as a dark age. Yet I am convinced that several centuries from now in the retrospect of history it is bound to be recognized as such, in spite of all its admitted accomplishments in the area of the natural. We really have lost a genuine capacity which the rest of mankind has possessed and actively exercised, and we have become a people trapped and in bondage within the prison of space, time, and matter. The achievements which make this the golden age of science have led to this imprisonment and made it at the same time a dark age.

Consider, for example, the contrast between the world of Shakespeare and Goethe at the dawn of science and our present day. Surely much has been gained in the interval by way of insight into the structure of nature and the laws by which nature is governed. Doubtless there were many superstitions, errors, and unnecessary fears then which science has by now largely dispelled. But just as surely much more has been lost by way of access to all that lies beyond nature. We are today still ardent advocates of the arts—music, poetry, and painting—but they have now become no more than outward expressions of an inner world of the artist's subjective emotional experience and lively imagination. The external reference in supernatural reality has vanished, and there is nothing left to express but a subjective world inside man himself. America today is said to be quite religious and the post-war religious revival is frequently cited in support of this contention. But at the same time religion is quite generally regarded throughout our culture as a purely private and inner manifestation of man's subjective experience, possessing no external reference in objective reality. Much is said these days about the importance of values. Because, however, there is nothing discoverable by science within the world of nature in which any value system could be rooted, the only seat for values which remains is within man himself. Thus we live in a culture for which the arts, religion, and values would vanish from the universe should man perish from it. This is the dark age, the bondage to the natural, the imprisonment within the limited domain of space, time, and matter of which we have been speaking.

Against this briefly portrayed background of the character of our contemporary dark age, let us consider some of the implications for theology. Of primary importance is the difficulty which such an age experiences with the great supernatural events which constitute the heart of the Gospel: the Incarnation, Resurrection, and Ascension of Jesus Christ. So long as the material universe in space and time was quite naturally thought of as immersed in a larger reality, the event in which the Son of God "came down from heaven, and was incarnate by the Holy Ghost of the Virgin Mary, and was made man" could acquire its central place in the scheme of things as a real event in the real history of this world. But in our age even the bare idea of heaven as a real mode of existence transcendent to the space-time continuum has been largely lost. Viewed from within the prison of the modern scientific age, no transcendent domain of reality exists out of which the divine Word could come into space and time and be made flesh. In such a restricted framework of reality, the Incarnation is simply impossible as a real event. Even those who accept its truth propositionally often experience difficulty in giving it substantial meaning within the framework of reality as they conceive it.

Bishop Robinson expresses this difficulty quite explicitly in his book, *Honest to God*, to which we have already referred. At the outset he announces that "the entire conception of a supernatural order which invades and 'perforates' this one must be abandoned" (p. 24). Thereafter the non-reality of supernature is repeatedly asserted in full conformance to the contemporary style of thought. When applied to the Incarnation this non-reality leads him to a series of questions which constitute a clear denial of the doctrine: "But suppose the whole notion of 'a God' who 'visits' the earth in the person of 'his Son' is as mythical as the prince in the fairy story? Suppose there is no realm 'out there' from which the 'Man from heaven' arrives? Suppose the Christmas myth (the invasion of 'this side' by 'the other side')—as opposed to the Christmas history (the birth of the man, Jesus of Nazareth)—has to go? Are we prepared for that?" It is clear from such statements from a bishop, nurtured in the Church throughout his entire life, that the secret imaginative framework which colours the contemporary style of thought affects our entire culture. It operates on those within the Church just as much as on those without.

We are all aware of the widespread difficulty which the Resurrection presents to the modern mind. The key to an understanding of the real source of this difficulty is the recognition of the extent to which our age is imprisoned in space, time, and matter. It is clear from all of the accounts in the New Testament of the post-resurrection appearances that Christ was raised into a new state of being no longer subject to the limitations of His earlier incarnate existence in the flesh. The resurrection is a very different event from the raising of Lazarus, who was only restored to this mortal existence for a brief additional period, and in time had to die again. The risen Christ, however, could appear and disappear at will, even in closed rooms, and thus had been raised out of death into a mode of existence no longer confined, as we are, to three-dimensional space and time. As so many of the Easter hymns proclaim, the resurrection was a bursting forth from the prison of space, time, and matter into a wider, freer, and eternal mode of existence.

Much the same can be said of the Ascension. To the contemporary mind, which we have seen has become largely incapable of conceiving any real transcendent or supernatural mode of existence, the Ascension can be interpreted, if at all, only as an event within space and time. In such a framework it cannot, of course, be regarded as an actual event, and so must be demythologized, as Bultmann has in fact done, in order to make it acceptable to contemporary thought. But actually the Ascension is in fact Christ's final translation out of space and time. Instead of a movement upwards in ordinary space, it was a translation outwards along a perpendicular, if you wish, to three-dimensional space and time. During the forty days of His risen life, He moved freely into and out of our world. The Ascension is not essentially different in character from any of the previous instances of His disappearance. It was simply that then the disciples knew that He would not return again in the body, but would thereafter be free to be supernaturally present in the breaking of bread everywhere and always whenever and wherever the Holy Eucharist was celebrated.

A striking commentary on what the scientific age has done to imprison the mind and spirit of man is provided by the contrasting responses of two Russian leaders to the results of missions carried out under their direction. In the tenth century Vladimir of Kiev sent emissaries to Constantinople where they experienced the supernatural power of the divine liturgy in Justinian's Church of the Holy Wisdom. They returned to report to him: "We thought we were in heaven; for it is impossible to find so much magnificence on earth. We believe that we were there in the presence of God and that the worship of other countries is totally eclipsed." Vladimir had himself and the people of Russia baptized, and the Russian Church was established. In the twentieth century another leader, Khrushchev, sent Major Titov and other emissaries on another mission in search of heaven, but this time high above the earth into orbits around it. They returned to report to him that there is really no heaven and no angels, only more of the same kind of space and matter as we have here. Krushchev is urgently engaged in using this mission as a means to disassociate his people from the Russian Church. In the intervening centuries, the world of nature has been vastly opened up to man's apprehension, but in the process he has almost completely lost his former easy access to the world of supernature.

It is difficult for us who are immersed in the spirit of our age to differentiate between the positive achievements of science and the restrictive pattern of beliefs and ways of looking at things which have grown with the rise of science and solidified into the twentieth-century style of thought. It is indeed not at all surprising that this should be the case. Science has produced revolutionary changes in our world view. Large areas of external reality previously regarded as supernatural are now solidly and definitely in the realm of nature. Many phenomena in the natural realm previously regarded as having supernatural causes are now understood scientifically within the framework of natural causation. In a very brief period of human history major reorientations and readjustments in established notions about the world and the place of man in it have been forced upon us. It is small wonder that great difficulties are being experienced between theology and science in the face of such revolutionary reorientations.

As I see it, the primary need is to recover a sense of the existence of a realm of supernature as a genuine part of external reality which is everywhere and always in immediate contact with the realm of nature. In the contemporary dark age this is exceedingly difficult to do. So much that used to be regarded as supernature has vanished by incorporation into nature that many persons suppose that science has positively established the non-existence of any supernatural realm whatever. But this is clearly not the case. When I am working or thinking as a physicist, I am automatically confined to objects or phenomena in three-dimensional space and time. Whatever reality transcendent to space and time there may be, I would not even know where to begin to observe or explore it by the methods of physics. The whole theoretical structure of modern physics is spatio-temporal. Every discovery of some new particle or anti-particle or of some new phenomenon is a discovery of some aspect of nature previously unknown. Every advance in physics is ultimately a way of comprehending patterns of objects and events in space and time in some larger or more general perspective. Science is by definition the study of nature. It possesses no means whatever of deciding either for or against any aspect of external reality which transcends the realm of nature. If the realm of supernature exists at all it must be known and experienced in ways which lie wholly outside the scope of science.

An analogy which I have found most helpful for recovering a sense of the reality of supernature as well as its relationship to nature is provided by a small book of the last century by an English mathematician, Edwin Abbott, with the title, *Flatland*. It is a story about a two-dimensional universe of infinite extent. Throughout the story three-dimensional observers from spaceland are able to see, as the flatlanders cannot, how the whole of flatland is immersed in space. For the flatlanders the natural order is the sum total of objects and events in their two-dimensional domain. Everything else is for them supernatural. A sphere which visits flatland can enter or leave it at will at any point in it simply by moving perpendicular to the plane which constitutes the flatland universe. When he does, his "natural" component from the flatlander vantage point is the circle of his intersection with this plane. The rest of the sphere is his supernatural component.

The significance of *Flatland* lies in its capacity to awaken in a modern reader the thought that his own three-dimensional universe might be immersed in a larger, though invisible, reality in a way analogous to that in which flatland is immersed in space. It is effective in causing its readers to question the prevailing assumption that the visible domain of three-dimensional space constitutes the totality of all real existence external to man. Moreover, it provides a far more suitable framework on which to hang the universal human experiences of supernatural reality than does the prescientific picture of a supernatural realm up in the sky populated by non-material stars, planets, sun, and moon. Heaven is no longer either "up there" or "out there," as Bishop Robinson puts it, but perpendicular to and in immediate contact with every point in space. Such a framework is directly applicable to the sense of the immediacy and all pervasiveness of the divine presence which is so powerfully expressed in the 139th Psalm. Indeed, this sense of all natural things and places being aglow, as it were, with supernatural overtones is much more prominent in biblical thought than is the "three-story" cosmology with God and heaven "up there" which Israel simply shared with the rest of the ancient world.

The use of *Flatland* in this way is of course only an analogy and doubtless cannot be pushed too far. An even more direct and convincing way, perhaps, to modern man's recovery of a sense of the reality of that which transcends the natural order is provided by Rudolf Otto's classic, *The Idea of the Holy*. This book surveys the whole of mankind's experience of the holy in many different cultures and settings. It is a scholarly piece of work carried out in a spirit and an approach which are entirely agreeable to the modern scientific style of thought. Yet the sheer universality and integrity of what Otto calls *numinous* experience becomes convincing evidence that one is here dealing with an elemental human capacity for experiencing and knowing reality beyond oneself. The object of the numinous experience, which Otto effectively calls the *mysterium tremendum*, seems to be as definite a part of external reality as rocks

and trees and atoms. Underneath all the errors and superstitions which have grown up around this category of experience, there is something *real* which only an age that
dogmatically rejects all supernatural reality could fail to
grasp.

I have dealt at greater length with both these approaches
in my book, *Physicist and Christian.* This brief account will
have to suffice here. At this point I wish to turn to a related
question, namely, the interaction of the supernatural with
the natural. More specifically, I wish to consider the reality
of God's action in a universe governed by scientific laws
and the related question of divine providence in its biblical
sense. This matter I have dealt with at length in another
book, *Chance and Providence.* Here we have to do with
the dominant conviction of modern thought that the explanation for everything which happens in space and time
is to be found within space and time. In its extreme form
this conviction expresses itself in mechanistic determinism.
But even those who would explicitly reject a thoroughgoing
mechanical determination of events are still likely to feel
that the only real causes are natural causes, and that whatever explanation there may be for events in nature must be
sought within nature. In contrast the biblical view sees the
whole natural order, the world and its history, as continu-
ously responsive to the will and purpose of its creator, so
that the explanation for the course of history must be sought
in such categories as grace, judgment, redemption, providence.

The key to a coalescence of the scientific view and the
biblical view lies in achieving a proper perspective on the
character of the general laws of nature and the part they
play in the shaping of events. Most people, I am convinced,
have an erroneous view of the way in which the scientific
laws operate. It is a view derived mainly from the character and expectations of nineteenth-century science and

modelled on the sure and accurately predictable motions of the planets and their satellites. It conceives of the laws of nature as rigorously determining the course which any system in the universe must follow in each of its individual components. Actually, however, throughout the whole range of the sciences from physics through biology to psychology and sociology, the laws of nature as they are now known and formulated are almost entirely statistical in character. There are generally several alternative modes of response in the same situation, and the laws of science govern the probabilities of each of them. A familiar example is life insurance in which life expectancies or the probability of death by any given age can be accurately predicted, but the time of death in individual cases cannot.

Because of this statistical character of scientific law, the best that can be done through science is to predict the most probable course of events. Divine providence in its biblical sense, however, manifests itself chiefly in those crucial turning points at which history takes a most improbable turn. The boundary between the natural and the supernatural determinants of history is formed by chance and accident. So long as things go rather much as expected, everything seems quite natural and dependable. But the really great and decisive moments in which the major achievements of life and history are made are just those which were least expected and most surprising in their occurrence. It is precisely in such events that God's action manifests itself and we are made aware of a divine purpose mysteriously working itself out in history. Such events do not violate natural laws. They are simply so improbable or so accidental as to be essentially indeterminate and unpredictable in terms of the laws of nature.

A comment of the distinguished physicist, J. Robert Oppenheimer, in his Reith lectures is relevant here: "We think . . . of general laws and broad ideas as made up of the instances which illustrate them, and from an observation of which we may have learned them. Yet this is not the whole. The individual event, the act, goes far beyond the general law. It is a sort of intersection of many generalities, harmonizing them in one instance as they cannot be harmonized in general."[1]

We often fail to appreciate how highly artificial are the situations in science in which the regularities of nature are revealed. Each experiment in which some law of nature is verified represents great ingenuity and highly developed technical skill on the part of the scientist performing it. It must exclude a variety of extraneous influences which are always present in the natural, non-laboratory situation. It rigorously restricts what may happen to precisely that controlled sequence of events in which the particular law, and no other, is operative. In the individual event or act in history, however, many separate trains of causal sequences intersect, as Oppenheimer says. Complex apparatus would be required in the laboratory to isolate each such sequence from the others so as to see what general laws were operative in that aspect of the total event. The laws are all there and operative in the complex fabric of the total situation. But in the event itself, they are all gathered at a particular moment and harmonized by that gathering in the achievement of the end which in retrospect the event is seen to have brought about. It is only in that harmony that the total reality of both the natural and the supernatural domains becomes evident. The supernatural dimension remains invisible and empirically inaccessible. But if it were not there as an integral determinant of the total event, there would be no harmony.

My purpose in this lecture has been to attempt to bring out the way in which the problem of theology and science

[1] J. Robert Oppenheimer, *Science and the Common Understanding* (New York, 1953), p. 93.

in our time is basically a problem of the style of thought characteristic of our age. We are to a greater or lesser extent victims of that secret imaginative framework of thought which our culture has instilled in us from infancy and which colours our whole outlook. Within the bondage of that framework, theology—with its concentration on the structure of supernatural reality, its categories of grace, sin, and providence, its insistence on the actuality and key importance of supernatural events in history, such as the Incarnation, Resurrection, and Ascension—seems unreal, alien to the spirit of the age, and without any valid reference in external reality. Yet if modern man only finds the way to recover his lost capacity of response to reality transcendent to space, time, and matter, all this could be changed. It is possible then to imagine a liberated and less restrictive mode of thought in which both theology and science have full range and scope—the one illuminating the character of supernature and the other the character of nature.

My venture into Christian theology is relatively recent, being confined exclusively to the past dozen years of my life. Prior to that, I was completely immersed in the scientific community and my outlook on any question completely dominated by the scientific habit of mind. In the early part of this venture theology was of course for me a whole new thought world. My reaction then to this new world was centred chiefly around the resolution of what seemed at first to be conflicts between science and theology. The more I have wrestled with these supposed conflicts, however, the more I have become aware of that secret imaginative framework of thought which was colouring the way in which I dealt with every question. The whole experience has been one of a growing sense of liberation from a too restrictive way of looking at things. It is something comparable to the exhilarating sense of release which early men of the Renaissance experienced. I covet this same kind of liberation for university students today, particularly because it is primarily the business of the university to maintain and transmit the contemporary mode and style of thought and so to maintain the imprisonment of our time. It saddens me to see a new generation being victimized by this all pervasive spirit of this epoch.

I have been impressed with the extent to which others with a history similar to my own have emerged with much the same sense of having been victimized by the style of thought instilled in them by their culture. The English historian, Herbert Butterfield, having been immersed for so long in the secular, non-transcendental spirit which pervades contemporary academic history, reflects this same viewpoint when in the concluding pages of his profound book, *Christianity and History*, he says:

In these days when people are so much the prisoners of systems —especially the prisoners of those general ideas which mark the spirit of the age—it is not always realized that belief in God gives us greater elasticity of mind, rescuing us from too great subservience to intermediate principles, whether these are related to nationality or ideology or science. . . . There are times when we can never meet the future with sufficient elasticity of mind, especially if we are locked in the contemporary systems of thought. We can do worse than remember a principle which both gives us a firm Rock and leaves us the maximum elasticity for our minds: the principle: Hold to Christ, and for the rest be totally uncommitted.[2]

We shall see, I believe, during the remainder of this century increasing numbers of scholars in all fields making this same kind of discovery of the intellectual and spiritual bondage of contemporary thought. As they do, the climate in our universities will slowly change. Already in physics and astronomy the contingency of space-time on that which

[2]Herbert Butterfield, *Christianity and History* (New York, 1950) pp. 145, 146.

transcends it is beginning to be sensed more and more frequently. The elementary particles of matter seem to depend for their particular observable properties on abstract mathematical entities which lie outside space and time. As the history of the universe is pushed backwards in time, one seems to come to a beginning at which space, time, and matter all come into existence together. This is gradually modifying traditional ways of thinking about physical reality. In biological science the transformation of patterns of thought is likely to come much later, but in the end it is, I believe, inevitable. The initial and entirely justified enthusiasm over the discovery of the genetic code and the manner of information storage and retrieval in living cells will require some time to run its course. But in time the essentially providential and purposeful character of the long history of the elaboration of DNA codes from the first living things to the production of man will be increasingly perceived.

In the humanities as well as the sciences one sees signs of change in patterns of thought. The domination of both history and philosophy by rigidly scientific categories is showing signs of weakening. In this situation a new university, such as York, has, it seems to me, a very special opportunity. Professor Butterfield and an increasing company of scholars in all fields form the vanguard of an exciting movement of recovery of lost treasures in our heritage. York as it builds and grows can seize the initiative by making this movement an integral part of its educational programme. Already a highly significant start has been made in Professor Kilbourn's course in the humanities with its strong emphasis on the Judaeo-Christian root of Western culture. I have been most impressed with the selection and quality of material in this course and the imaginative way in which it strikes at the heart of the problem we have been considering. This kind of educational experience is rare in modern university curricula. In offering such experience, York is exercising significant leadership in an important educational area. It is my hope that as future units of the university are built, this lead can be further developed and expanded.

What is important is to share our Judaeo-Christian heritage with students in a way which makes it clear that it is concerned with external reality just as much as is science. Too often it seems to the students to be associated with an outmoded and discredited world view. In that case no matter how moving and powerful its literary treasures may be, it does not seem to the students to represent genuine knowledge. Only as it is seen to provide genuine insight into the character of supernatural reality does it become exciting and relevant to modern man. This achievement is difficult in the contemporary world, but it only makes the task all the more challenging. There is so much pressure for conformity to accepted canons of inquiry in every academic community, so great a tendency to pass on to the next generation the same style and system of thought in which the present generation is already trapped, that few institutions are likely to rise to this challenge. York has shown admirable courage and perception in blazing a trail into this largely untouched territory. As this programme grows with the rise of the new campus, it could prove to be the most significant thing the university has done. If, as I believe, we are in a dark age and a renaissance of recovery of lost capacities of response to reality is now under way, though largely hidden, the university which takes the leadership in participating in this renaissance will in time stand out as a great centre of renewal. That is an exciting prospect.

There is, however, more involved in this renewal than curriculum and courses. The fullness of our Judaeo-Christian heritage cannot be realized in purely "intellectual and scholarly activities." Both in Judaism and in Christianity the centre of the religious life is a community—Israel in the one, the Church in the other. The deepest expression of the access to supernatural reality which is realized in these communities is to be found in their corporate worship. Here the truth of what is being taught in the classroom is experienced as fact. The primary barrier in the way of adding this component to the total educational experience offered by a university is the religious diversity and fragmentation of the Church in the modern world. The oecumenical movement, now surging forward, will hopefully in time heal many of the old wounds and remove some of the barriers which now divide Christians. This process however, will certainly be prolonged.

In the meantime it would seem that York University has a special opportunity to meet this problem in a unique and especially effective way. There are to be, as I understand it, some twelve or more colleges on the new campus on which construction is to start soon. Would it be possible for a few of these to be set aside for students who wished to live in their own religious community within the larger academic community? There could be a Roman Catholic, an Anglican, a Protestant, and a Jewish college as a minimum. This would still leave an adequate number of purely secular colleges for the large number of students who would prefer them. If this could be done, the various churches would doubtless provide a priest or rabbi of adequate academic stature to serve as chaplain or master of their college. The students of such a college would share the corporate life and worship in their own tradition and in addition would be assisted greatly in understanding their general university courses in the light of that tradition. Such an arrangement seems to me to have considerable potentiality, and I would like to commend it to you for serious consideration.

It would be a mistake to expect dramatic results from this programme. The patterns of thought and basic presupposi-

tions which characterize our present culture are deeply im-
bedded and change very slowly. At first only a few students
will be reached in depth by this programme. But for the
few who are, it is an exciting and liberating experience. They
become a part of that small core within the university who
are sensitive to the winds of change, and know themselves
to be participants in a gradual process of recovery of man's
age-old capacity of response to transcendent reality. Imper-
ceptibly but surely in the years ahead the secret imaginative
background which determines the intellectual climate in our
universities is changing. As this change progresses, an ever-
increasing segment of our culture will find itself freed from
our contemporary bondage to space, time, and matter, and
enjoying a recovered capacity of response to those ranges
of reality which transcend the order of nature. This is the
vision and the goal which must continue to support the
promising programme you have initiated here at York
University.

God's Angry Men

Maurice N. Eisendrath

Maurice N. Eisendrath

Maurice N. Eisendrath is President, Union of American Hebrew Congregations, the parent body of Reform Judaism in the Western Hemisphere. Rabbi Eisendrath, a graduate of the University of Cincinnati, was ordained as Rabbi in 1926 at Hebrew Union College. He has served in this capacity at the Virginia Street Temple, Charleston, West Virginia, and at the Holy Blossom Temple, Toronto, Canada. Rabbi Eisendrath is author of The Never Failing Stream.

BEFORE embarking on my theme of "God's Angry Men," I think that you, faculty, students, governors, friends of York University, might be interested to hear of a singular coincidence upon which I stumbled this past summer in London. I was reading the London *Times* and, after exhausting all the details of the "affaire Profumo," I turned to the editorial page. There, in the lead editorial, I read some words of uninhibited commendation of a small university which was located in what was apparently to the editor as well as to his readers some unfamiliar provincial town known as Toronto.

This editorial confessed that it was perfectly conceivable that a forthcoming Conference of British Universities "might well dispel any notion that we [in Britain] will confer more benefit on the visitors than on our home-bred academics." In a surprising mood of British literary humility, the editorial admitted: "We stand to profit, too. We are so used to exporting scholarship that some people could be forgiven, perhaps, for supposing that Britain is the [sole or principal] repository of what wise experience there is about University affairs." And then transcending the insularity usually associated with Great Britain, it continued: "In fact, some of the most progressive thinking on the work and nature of Universities is already being done overseas." I was dumbfounded. My preconceptions and prejudices concerning British academic hauteur—especially of the "Ox-Bridge" variety—were dissipated.

But I was especially fascinated by the genesis of this editorial, the particular example which had evoked these unusually effusive statements, for, in the very next line I discovered the name of a university of whose existence I—living but a few hundred miles away—had not even known until but a few months before when I received an invitation to speak at one of its lecture series. The editorial had these most complimentary words for this university: "What English Foundation, as young as York [University, Toronto, Canada] has produced such admirable cogitation?" Such "admirable cogitation" was further referred to as that "distinguished book which has come from its President, Dr. Murray Ross, on *The New University*." Equally worthy of acclaim is the second publication, *The University and the New World*, from which the *Times* quoted these searching words, spoken by Professor Howard Mumford Jones of Harvard University: "If a university has any unique purpose that no other institution can quite fulfil it is, or should be as a place for weighing fundamental thoughts. They also serve who only stand and think. Indeed, it may be less important for a university to have a cyclotron than it is to have a soul."

Evidently, York concurs with Professor Jones's viewpoint and is turning its attention this year to finding that soul—of the university, of the world, of man himself. And so you would have me speak of "Religion and the University," to essay, in your President's words of guidance to me, "to find some explanation for, perhaps even some antidote to, the increased alienation evident among our young people"—their interest in existentialism, the hostility of many to the Church, the frequently heard argument that the Church is not related to the real problem of the world today.

This is a tough assignment, indeed, and one for which, without any false modesty, I feel all too inadequately equipped. Our age is not so simple as Hillel's, nor are our university students quite so simple-minded as the stranger who came to that ancient rabbi's door and demanded a delineation of religion while he stood on one foot. Simpleminded denizen of a simple, uncomplicated era, he seemed satisfied with Hillel's reply: "Do not do unto another what you would not have him do unto you." But we live in a highly complex age when none of us can fail to feel utterly inadequate because of our incapacity to grasp even the barest rudiments of most of the disciplines of our day. A Hillel could. So could a Socrates, a Plato, an Aristotle. Even as late as the Middle Ages, the Jewish philosopher, Maimonides, could become a widely renowned physician, attending rulers and princes and people, and at the same time be one of the profoundest thinkers and most erudite writers of his time. It is not so today. Who knows enough of physics, mathematics, medicine, electronics, computers, the depths of the seas, the infinite stretches of space—to say nothing of human behaviour and a "religion relevant to our time"? Here is a whole new world in which none can master all its convolutions, planes, and directions. We can only be overwhelmed by inferiority complexes, especially as we viewed those recent famous—or infamous—quiz shows or watch still today such contests of factual data as "College Bowl" and similar exhibitions of the endless variety and vastness of contemporary information. Surely in the face of all this, the subject given me—to provide, in a brief space of time, an answer to the doubts, the questioning, the search-ing of a whole generation of college youth—cannot but make me feel totally inadequate.

Nevertheless, I believe, just a clue to an answer to the problem of "Religion and the University" may be found both in the still lingering, ancient misconceptions of religion as well as—paradoxically enough—in some of the more recently and cleverly contrived neo-orthodoxies which are as illusory and as misleading as the outmoded blinkers of the past. As to the first, I am reminded of a symposium held at Massey Hall when I engaged in a discussion with the late Clarence Darrow on religion. At first I did not dream of mentioning such ancient history tonight. But

when I find that such wavelengths as are assigned—none too
generously—on radio and television to religious broadcast-
ing are largely the monopoly of the primitivist, hell-and-
brimstone-breathing evangelists, I feel the need to spend a
moment or two, not in lamenting, but in applauding whatever student revolt there may be against this shadow rather
than substance of religion. For Darrow had held up this
same antiquated religious teaching as the target of his
scathing attack. He anticipated Mr. Khrushchev's cynical
conclusion that his cosmonauts had, at long last, searched
the heavens and combed the sky but had not seen God.
Who ever said God was to be *seen*, except the rankest of
idolators—pagan, Christian, or Jew?

So Darrow also inquired: Did any scientist ever find God
in his microscope? Of course none has, but most of today's
scientists—humbler than those of Darrow's time, than Darrow himself—do agree that though God may not be found
under the miscroscope's lens, at least there are intimations
of His presence revealed by the most recent scientific probings into the long-hidden secrets of the universe. They
concur in the findings of Professor Theodosius Dobzhansky
of Columbia University who, in commenting on the uniqueness of man, has written:

> The human body starts its existence as a fertilized egg cell,
> weighing about one-twenty millionth of an ounce. An adult is
> some fifty billion times heavier. The growth occurs through
> assimilation of food. Quite literally, man is a conglomeration of
> transformed groceries. And yet, this conglomeration is alive,
> feels joy and suffering, is conscious of self, and of the existence
> of other persons and of the universe. In the words of one of the
> Dead Sea Scrolls: "So walk I on uplands unbounded, and know
> that there is hope, for that which Thou didst mold out of dust
> to have consort with things eternal."[1]

[1]Theodosius Dobzhansky, "Genetics and the Destiny of Man," *Pro-
ceedings of the X International Congress of Genetics,* vol. I (Toronto,
1959), p. 468.

But can a complexity so great, and yet so orderly, as man arise simply from an arrangement of atoms in the materials which are kept on the shelves of grocery stores? Dr. Dobzhansky's answer is both yes and no. Nothing from the outside has supernaturally, artificially entered into man. But today's scientists do find evidence throughout the long chain of evolution that things altogether unprecedented and unanticipated occur and that man has developed a nature— a spiritual nature, if you please—an equation, a dimension not opposed by the scientists of our time, a dimension which these scientists do not hesitate to call the spirit of man who "stands with one foot in his biological past and with the other in his divine future."

"The spirit of man is the light of the Lord," chanted the psalmist centuries ago. And George Russell Harrison, Dean of the School of Science at the Massachusetts Institute of Technology, writes:

It is not difficult for a scientist to see the hand of God in the patterns which protons, neutrons, and electrons take in forming atoms, and those which the atoms take to form molecules, molecules to form cells, cells to form tissues, organs, and bodies, and bodies to form social aggregates. . . . The basic tenets of all great religions, the distilled spiritual wisdom of humanity, coincide closely with what science reveals in nature.[2]

Even such an incorrigible scoffer as George Bernard Shaw had far greater appreciation of religion's capacity to survive the microscope's penetrating eye, the x-ray's probing, the telescope, or even the astronaut's soaring through space. For Shaw, like his fellow satirist, Darrow, though he devoted a good part of his life to the task of tearing to shreds the blind superstitions of his day, that men might see more clearly the light of truth so long obscured by the

[2]George Russell Harrison, *The Role of Science in Our Modern World* (Apollo eds., New York, 1956), pp. 231, 244. This book was originally published under the title *What Man May Be: The Human Side of Science.*

dust and cobwebs of fable, myth, and legend, had at least the candour to admit that one cannot that easily dispose of religion as revealed in a profounder understanding of the Bible. In his attack on all orthodoxies, in that quaint and absorbing little fantasy entitled *The Adventures of the Black Girl in Her Search for God*, Shaw remarked:

A great deal of the Bible is much more alive than this morning's paper and last night's parliamentary debate. Its chronicles are better reading than most of our fashionable histories, and less intentionally mendacious. In revolutionary invective and Utopian aspiration it cuts the ground from under the feet of Ruskin, Carlyle, and Karl Marx; and in epics of great leaders and great rascals it makes Homer seem superficial and Shakespear unbalanced. And its one great love poem is the only one that can satisfy a man who is really in love. Shelley's Epipsychidion is, in comparison, literary gas and gaiters.[3]

No truer word could be written, or spoken. Where is there a more revolutionary or relevant doctrine for our time than is to be found in Amos' passionate plea for justice, Isaiah's vision of a world at peace, and Hosea's appeal for compassion between man and his brother man?

But it is not the antiquarian fundamentalists who alone posit a false and outworn faith. They are today being echoed by the most modern of contemporary theologians who, weary of the search for certitude, overwhelmed by the complexity of our day, are seized with nostalgic yearnings for the "leeks and garlic" of outmoded orthodoxies of all kinds. They retreat into ivory towers of mystic obfuscations and take refuge in the storm cellars of irrationality and irresponsibility, thus prompting our present-day existentialists to liken man to "a race of worms" crawling about on an intellectual or spiritual opium pad in a flight from reality and responsibility to some sort of self-imposed narcosis.

[3]George Bernard Shaw, *The Adventures of the Black Girl in Her Search for God* (London, 1934), p. 11.

They surrender to such conclusions as Sartre's that there is "No Exit," or *Kein Ausweg*, as Kafka phrases it, no escape for man caught by the carapace of his alleged innate and inescapable evil, grovelling helplessly and hopelessly in his darkened cave unable to climb up and out unless God's ladder of salvation is magically lowered down to him.

It is as a consequence of both these trends of our time, the orthodox revival of primitive anti-intellectualism and the neo-orthodoxies of the contemporary pseudo-intelligentsia, that the business of religion is booming, temple and church budgets are soaring, membership rosters in existing congregations are mushrooming, new congregations are burgeoning on every hand. New religious structures are looming skyward, even if not actually heavenward, in what has been dubbed the greatest "edifice complex" in history. The pollsters tell us that the preacher is once again climbing back to the pedestal of his erstwhile pre-eminence from which he was so rudely catapulted by the businessman, the statesman (or rather the politician), and the scientist. Yes, indeed, whereas a survey conducted some years ago indicated that the clergyman was nearing the bottom of the list of popularly approved professions, a more recent poll revealed that a majority of our contemporaries conceded that "the ministry as a group is doing the most good and is the most to be trusted."

But what does all this really mean? Some fear that it may mean that we are confusing mere formal affiliation with genuine fealty and faith; that with all our multiplication of members and money and machinery to become, in the lingo of the beatnik, "big man, big," there may be less of the pursuit and practice of our prophetic preachment; that, as the President of Union Theological Seminary has phrased it, "while the curve of religious affiliation is rising, that of moral health is falling." Thus, there are those who are concerned that religion may be in the process of becoming too

popular in our fat and fatuous two-dimensioned society,
replacing other fashions and fads without forging for us a
light-bearing faith or a life-changing challenge; that God,
as someone has put it, has been converted into a kind of
"Honorary Chairman" of our vast and ubiquitous philan-
thropic syndrome, his ministers reduced to mere grace
notes and footnotes, "invocators" and "benedictors" at the
lavish banquets at which He is so servilely attended, and
religion, the Synagogue and the Church, looked upon as
instrumentalities to procure not what we need but what we
crave, "Comfort and Fun in a nice Society."

And so some of us—on campus and off—are beginning
to inquire whether religion, which has triumphed over every
trial of privation, can survive its present boom? Will its
voice continue to cry out clearly and courageously from
the midst of these costlier courts, or will it be stifled in a
kind of Chamber of Anaesthesia, satisfied with the status
quo, and content with these new hordes of status-seeking
suburbanites swarming into their houses of worship to be
"fed on the pap of our contemporary faith in faith"? And
all the while, blind though we be, we are breeding a generation of "way-out" cynical "cats" who care less for Amos'
cry for justice and Jesus' plea for compassion than they do
for Allen Ginsberg's "Howl," with its not altogether irre-
verent or irrelevant sermon on the text from Jeremiah:
"Lament and howl for the fierce anger of the Lord is upon
us"; upon all our complacent, cozy, country-club together-
ness of organization men. So lament and howl, as does
Ginsberg, as do all these disillusioned children of darkness
who stand in seeming bravado but in actual trembling and
terror before the reawakened gods of Mammon and Mars
and Moloch—that Moloch whom Ginsberg describes as
the Lord of

Solitude! Filth! Ugliness! Ashcans and unobtainable dollars!
Children screaming under stairways! Boys sobbing in armies!

Old men weeping in the parks! Moloch! Moloch! Nightmare of Moloch! Moloch the loveless! . . . Moloch the stunned governments! Moloch whose mind is pure machinery! Moloch whose blood is running money! Moloch whose fingers are ten armies! Moloch whose breast is a cannibal dynamo! . . . Moloch whose skyscrapers stand in the long streets like endless Jehovahs! . . . Moloch whose smokestacks and antennae crown the cities![4]

Here, at least, is a flash of welcome anger. Of course, I realize that anger is no longer in vogue. As a matter of fact, the designation "angry young men" which is usually employed to describe the youthful playwrights and poets, especially of Great Britain, is looked upon today with something of disdain and derogation. To some, this flight from anger may seem to herald the very dawn of Utopia. To those of us who were carefully taught in our childhood to mind our tongues and were punished for our temper tantrums and for any slightest exhibition of childhood rage, this particular absence of wrath in our time may seem to be the sure sign of emotional maturity. It may signalize the fact that we have become truly civilized. Only the "barbarians" remove their shoes in public, pound the desk, and rant and rave. We, however, remain complacent and composed: our pulse is normal, our blood pressure under rigid control, our passions unaroused. To be sure, for a moment or two we may feel some twinge of distress when we read about a race riot in South Africa or of the brutal bludgeoning of brother by brother in the United States. But we soon shrug our shoulders and return to our blood-and-thunder television westerns, our bridge tables, our baseball or hockey games or our tennis matches, unbothered or bored by world events or politics in this disinterested, alienated time which a contemporary social commentator describes as being subsumed in "one big yawn," as the "bland leading the bland."

Unhappily, this mood seems to have seized the once

[4]Allen Ginsberg, "Howl" in *Howl and Other Poems* (City Lights Books, San Francisco, 1956), p. 17.

volatile students—and faculties—of too many contemporary colleges, on this continent especially. Michael Novak writes, in a special issue of *Harper's Magazine* on "The College Scene":

... while Europe was torn nearly to its death by the ideological and physical contortions of recent revolutions and wars, America and England have tried earnestly to go on as before, as if nothing has happened. The war washed away the intellectual foundations of Europe's past, and intellectuals like Camus, Sartre, Marcel, Barth, and Guardini have fought desperately for intellectual starting points—whether they deny or affirm the possibility of religious faith. But in America and England, philosophy and art showed little such desperation; men tried to pick up where they had left off, a little more tired, a little more angry, worried about the bomb, but not fundamentally changed. ... The radicalism of the American thirties has been fragmented by prosperity. ...

... Even among the professors it is assumed that ultimate questions are nonintellectual, personal, and if matters of supreme importance and self-commitment, nevertheless not matters for passionate academic dispute. The university, on principle, concentrates on statistics, historical facts, historical intellectual positions, logic modeled on the discourse of the physical sciences, and ample documentation. Even the literature courses, under the impact of the New Criticism, have the students noting the occurrences of words, running down allusions, and abstracting from the conditions of history. The Anglo-American university has committed itself to all that is "objective," countable, precise, publicly verifiable. Though this commitment suits the middle-class temper capitally, it stifles religion almost to death.

Not only religion is stifled. More fundamentally, it is possible —it is even common—for a student to go to class after class of sociology, economics, psychology, literature, philosophy, and the rest, and hardly become aware that he is dealing with issues of life and death, of love and solitude, of inner growth and pain. He may never fully grasp the fact that education is not so much information and technique as self-confrontation and change in his own conscious life. He may sit through lectures and write examinations—and the professors may *let* him do merely that— collecting verbal "answers," without really thinking through and

deciding about any new aspect of his own life in any course. . . .
. . . "You've got to teach these youngsters to forget the
shoulds and *musts* they came here with," one new teaching fellow was recently admonished by his program director. "The
students have to learn to be objective." And of course such a
critique is excellent, since some *shoulds* and *musts* are what a
man dies for. . . . [But in the words of Professor Ralph Demos
of Harvard] the colleges make a "commitment to noncommit-
ment," have a "faith in non-faith."[5]

Small wonder that the erstwhile restiveness of youth
which once caused young people almost invariably to be,
at least for a time, in angry revolt against the previous
generation, is apparently passé, as too many college students appear to be satisfied with panty pilfering, crowding
into telephone booths, burning park benches, or pushing
beds around. We are thus constrained to give at least some
semblance of belief to William Whyte's conclusion in the
The Organization Man that there is a passivity today about
youth. No cause seizes them. "The last thing students can
be accused of now is dangerous discussion; they are not
interested in the kind of big questions that stimulate
heresy."[6] They are, in fact, somewhat bored by it all.

It was not always so. My Jewish, and many of your
Christian forbears, envisaged a "God of wrath"—not the
"God of vengeance" who supposedly looked with approval
upon the bashing of banies and sought the blood of one's
enemies, but the God of anger when wrong was perpetrated
and justice was denied. Now I must confess that a God of
anger and wrath seems painfully pagan and primitive in this
later day of super-sophistication. But I wonder whether we
would have preferred that God had remained smilingly and
indifferently indulgent as men continued to "join house to
house and field to field," as they "sold the needy for a pair

[5]Michael Novak, "God in the Colleges," *Harper's Magazine*, Oct.
1961, pp. 174, 175.
[6]William Whyte, *The Organization Man* (New York, 1956), p. 72.

of shoes," fed not the hungry, clothed not the naked, and took not the homeless to their habitation? Or whether it was not preferable that God should have expressed His great anger through those angry men such as the prophet Isaiah, who likewise called upon his generation to howl for "the fierce anger of the Lord is kindled against you because of the multitude of your transgressions," or Jesus, who, despite his gentleness, did not fail, in righteous indignation and wrath, to drive the iniquitous money changers from the temple?

The founders of Canada were also angry men, God's angry men in revolt against the diminution and denial of freedom in the land from which they came. The Pilgrim pioneers, who came to the rock bound coasts of New England and later found their way to this land of Canada, did not cynically dismiss the difference between dictatorship and democracy as did a college student who maintained that "one vote more or less makes no difference," and concluded that "anyway I'm fed up with all this political jazz." Rather, the Pilgrim fathers and those who, a little less than one hundred years ago, drew up the articles of Canadian Confederation, came to these shores with the words "Rebellion to Tyrants is Obedience to God" ringing on their lips.

It seems to me that that anger, that righteous wrath, that moral indignation, which once characterized our God and His prophets needs to be revived; needs to be revived, not merely among the beatnik generation who cry out with Alan Ginsberg, but among the whole of our contemporary population and particularly among the youth of this too dispassionate generation. There is much today that ought to arouse our anger as we stand in the very shadow of the mushroom cloud and the fiery missiles. I realize that no one can agree on precisely how much deadly poison there may be in the present rate of nuclear fallout, but I do know that most authorities concur that, even if not a single additional

bomb is exploded, there are presently enough such poisons
to pollute and to destroy countless generations yet unborn.
Should not our anger ring in righteous indignation against
thus dooming even a single child of God? Should we not be
roused before those ghost-like figures I saw in Hiroshima
and Nagasaki with faces and hands swollen and scarred and
scorched, with great sheets of skin torn away from their
bones—like rags upon a scarecrow? Should we not insist,
in an era wherein this city is but fourteen minutes away
from Moscow by missile, that some greater effort still be
put forth in order to make quite certain that we, who are
born to be "but little lower than the angels," shall not be
constrained to scurry like rats beneath the earth and that
with our faith in a Universal Father we shall yet transcend
national sovereignty? Should we not be angered by our
tenacious clinging still to our childish immaturities? Are we
not the "foolish teen-age-minded tribes and sects" so aptly
described by Arnold Toynbee? Are we not, as Toynbee
reminds us, human beings before we are Russians or Ameri-
cans, capitalists or communists?

It appears to me that not only should there be a greater
degree of anger, wrath, and righteous indignation, not
merely in those bands of heroic and courageous Negro
youth and the small minority of their white colleagues, but
that all of us together ought to cry out to denounce to Hell
the whole miasma of racial hatred that besets our present
generation. At a time when a wild-eyed little coloured child
must walk through the Red Sea of hatred in order to reach
the Promised Land of the integrated school; when too many
in Canada as well as in the United States join the vigilantes
in seeking to safeguard the purity of our monochrome
neighbourhoods, our professions, our businesses from any
possible so-called "contamination" by those whom God's
brilliant sun has made somewhat darker than ourselves;
when bestiality breaks out, not merely in South Africa or

behind iron or bamboo curtains or in Cuba but upon this continent too against those who are seeking to carry out the edict both of a Supreme Court and of Him whom we call the Supreme Being; at such time, perhaps the words of Thoreau are most apt: "Under a government which imprisons any [person] unjustly, the true place for a just man is prison."[7] Surely we ought to be angry against all the hypocrisy which for generations has abused the Negro, or I should say the Negress, as a concubine and then has refused to grant equality to her offspring with the stupid, superficial jeer, "would you want your sister to marry a Negro." We forget that what the Negro wants to be is your brother and not your brother-in-law; he wants an end to that kind of hypocrisy which would ward him off with such a jibe and at the same time know, as the scientists reveal to us, that 22 per cent of the American so-called white population is the fruit of such backyard dalliances. It is time for anger *against* all such injustice and bigotry and *for* fellowship and love.

True religion, vital religion seeks "no pie in the sky" complacency; no patient "waiting for Godot"—or God either; no peace-of-mind palliative; no purveyors of unctuous pastor oil, massagers of souls, surrogates for the analyst's couch or the druggist's tranquilizers—but descendants of God's angry men, the prophets, not hesitating to go into the counting house or factory or governmental office and exclaim with Nathan: "Thou art the man!" It was said of Tolstoy that he "stabbed men awake." Is this not a time to "stab men awake"; to "light a spirit bomb" under our contemporaries who profess religion, to "jolt them out from under the husks of old dead meaning," a time when men need to be dynamited into wakefulness? In a world of shame we dare not slink supinely to the sidelines. "Jerusalem was destroyed," say our Hebrew sages, "because men

[7]Henry David Thoreau, *On the Duty of Civil Disobedience* (New American Library ed., New York, 1963), p. 230.

no longer rebuked each other." So will our world be destroyed if it hears only the salving syllables of those who pander after popularity rather than the scorpion sting of moral challenge.

Because this is a generation filled with what David Reisman in *The Lonely Crowd* describes as "Radar people" who, with no interalized goals, derive directions only from others, then surely it is incumbent upon us, upon religion, yes, and upon our universities which would "find their souls" to become those "others," *not* to walk a tightrope, not to sit Buddha-like on our thrones of Lotus leaves narcissistically contemplating our navels, to get along by going along; not to have our ears everlastingly to the ground, our eyes forever on the facial expressions of others, especially on those who can confer favours, fearful of every frown from those who would hire and fire us, quick to conform rather than to reform and transform, to comfort the afflicted but never to afflict the comfortable, frantically anaesthetizing our consciences by acquiring more of the world's goods instead of concerning ourselves with the good of the world, a "Cavalcade of dumb beasts, the head of one at the side of the other's tail."

This is the task of the university as well as of the Church —of a university which would find its soul and help save the soul of its students and of the world. As Michael Novak further states:

. . . If religion is to enter the university, it must enter first at the most elementary level: in experience, in awareness, in slow and gradual exploration. . . .
These experiences are often "prereligious"; they are barely starting points for full religious life. But they are the only foundation on which anything living can be built. I mean man's experience of his fragility, of his transitoriness, of his tininess; his consciousness of his uniqueness on the earth, of his endless and restless questioning; his peronal choices whose motives and consequences he cannot fully know; his vast ability to be proud

and to fail, to be isolated and to love, to be—and yet not to be —the master of his own destiny. . . .

If university teachers could right the balance, would religion begin to thrive? Those who have made faith central to their lives—who believe in the reality and relevance of God, and the interaction (in dark faith) of God and men—hold that it would. And if theology, as such, came to the campuses and became there embattled and truly controversial, this would be welcome; for the very fact that fundamental questions were posed would transform the experience of university life. . . .

One might have hoped that religious men within the secular colleges might by their understanding and their leadership have restored to American universities a chance for a living and critical experience of religion. . . But the strident tones of Fathers Feeney and Halton, and of William F. Buckley, Jr.'s essays and talks have sometimes soured the air. And for decades there have been too few men, at once intellectual and religious and wise on the campuses. Vast empty spaces seem to surround the Niebuhrs and the Tillichs. The churches are filled with worshipers but intelligence has fled from the ranks of religion. Who or what can bring it back?

What, then, is the place of God in our colleges? The basic human experiences that remind man that he is not a machine, and not merely a temporary cog in a technological civilization, are not fostered within the university. God is as irrelevant in the universities as in business organizations; but so are love, death, personal destiny. Religion can thrive only in a personal universe; religious faith, hope, and love are personal responses to a personal God. But how can the immense question of a personal God even be posed and made relevant when fundamental questions about the meaning and limits of personal experience are evaded?

"God is dead. . . . What are these churches if they are not the tombs and sepulchers of God?" Nietzsche asked. But much of Western humanism is dead too. Men do not wander under the silent stars, listen to the wind, learn to know themselves, question, "Where am I going? Why am I here?" They leave aside the mysteries of contingency and transitoriness, for the certainties of research, production, consumption. So that it is nearly possible to say: "Man is dead. . . . What are these buildings, these tunnels, these roads, if they are not the tombs and sepulchers of man?"

God, if there is a God, is not dead. He will come back to the colleges, when man comes back.[8]

That is, He will come back when man reaches out to his brother man and to God, when religion becomes not merely a guide to God but a goad to good. Whether in formal courses on the history of the world's great faiths or on comparative religion, or less formally in the search for relevant answers to the deepest questions of the individual and society, the university dare no longer retreat into its ivory —or ivied—towers, sundered from life; but hand in hand with Church and Synagogue, it must help to synthesize the discoveries of man's mind and the perplexities and probings of his soul.

The poet who wrote that "It is not good for man to dwell alone" had an intuitive psychological wisdom. The spiritual emphasis of Judaism upon corporate responsibility rather than upon individual salvation is amazingly prescient of what only now the mind of man is beginning to comprehend. Only "starry-eyed and deluded idealists" dared to share Judaism's belief in the indispensability of co-operation and in "separating not thyself from the community." Today, science, on the track at last of the source of cancer's scourge, has learned that its cause is to be found somewhere in the as yet unfathomed phenomenon which constrains certain cells to behave in an altogether individualistic manner, refusing to act in harmony with their disciplined fellow cells. And as the cells are to the body, so is the individual to society.

In the brotherhood of man, the university, the Church, and the world, the individual will find his soul and a religion relevant to life. This came poignantly home to me some years ago in a story I first heard when I was ministering in Canada. It is supposed to be a true story and it tells of a father, mother, and their children who were once crossing a

[8]Novak, "God in the Colleges," pp. 176, 177, 178.

vast wheat field in the Canadian west. The little child held each parent by the hand, walking between them. After they had gone along for some time in silence, the mother turned to the father and said, "Father, where is our child?" He looked down and he too discerned that it had evidently wandered off while they had been walking along absent-mindedly. Frantically, they searched this way and that but they could not find the child. They returned to their little village and called out all their neighbours and friends to assist them in the search. All that night and the following day and night they searched. On the morning of the third day they gathered around in a sad little group. Then one man hit upon a brilliant idea and he said to those gathered there: "Come, my friends, let us join hands, one to the other and form a human comb. We will thus cover the entire width of the field and we will march from one end of it to the other and surely thus we will find the missing child." They seized avidly upon his suggestion, and, joining hand to hand, they began their sombre march down the field. Suddenly, one man stumbled over an inert object, lifted it, placed it into the arms of the mother, who saw that her child was dead. And all that that grief-stricken mother could do was cry out of the depths of her desolation. "My God," she cried, "why did we not join hands sooner?" "My God" should be the ringing cry, even the angry cry of our generation. "My God, why do we not join hands, nation to nation, race to race, creed to creed, man with his brother man, before it is too late?"

> God give us men! A time like this demands
> Strong minds, great hearts, true faith, and ready hands;
> Men whom the lust of office does not kill;
> Men whom the spoils of office cannot buy;
> Men who possess opinions and a will;
> Men who have honor; men who will not lie.[9]

[9]Josiah Gilbert Holland (died 1881), "The Day's Demand."

Religion and the Importance of the Humanist Approach

Charles Moeller

Charles Moeller

Charles Moeller is Professor of Dogmatics and Literature in the Faculty of Philosophy and Letters, University of Louvain, Belgium, where he is also the Director of the Home Congolais. Following his studies at the Saint Boniface Institute in Brussels and the Seminary of Malines, Canon Moeller received his doctorate in theology from the University of Louvain in 1941. He is ecclesiastical policy adviser to the Oecumenical Council of the Roman Catholic Church. Canon Moeller's publications include Literature in the Twentieth Century and Christianity *and* Humanism and Holiness.

IN this first section I should like to describe the place and future of religion in society. Such an aim is undoubtedly surprising, for modern society seems to be irreligious. Certain people see one saving value in atheism, that it is "a humanism." To safeguard the freedom of science, to assure the political revolution by which men lives in the world, to transform the world, to save human dignity, we must abandon belief in God. "Moral conscience dies in contact with the absolute," wrote Merleau-Ponty. Renan, more than a century ago, published *The Future of Science*; Szesnick, a commentator on Radio Frankfurt, has just published a book entitled *The Future of Unbelief (Aberglauben)*; "God-Why?" is the title of one volume in the series *Jeunesse de l'Eglise*. God seems useless, even harmful. One is atheistic because one is a communist and a communist because atheistic, explains Le Diamat, the Marxist catechism. Marx had written: "Religion is the heart of a world without heart, the spirit of an age without spirit, it is the opium of the people."

Nothing of that has lingered on in the academic field. Pélagie Vlassovna, in the play *Mother Courage* which Brecht adapted from Gorki's novel, incarnates the unbelief of Marxist humanism. At first Pélagie had been ashamed of her son's revolutionary activities, but when she understood their meaning she associated herself with them. Thus she transcended the purely physical motherhood to attain what the Marxists call social motherhood. When, as too often happens once adolescence is passed, mothers are separated from, and more or less rejected by their sons, Pélagie is united to her son in common revolutionary activity by the mediation of the "third parent" (*dritte Sache*). The intervention of revolutionary activity reunites what blood and the psychological family invariably severs. Pélagie's son is shot dead when he tries to cross the Polish frontier. The women wish to console Pélagie Vlassovna. They offer her soup to nourish her body and a Bible to help her accept the inexplicable decree of Providence which has snatched away her son. Pélagie accepts the soup but refuses the Bible. "My son," she says, "was not killed by an inexplicable design of Providence, but by an explicable decree of the Tsar. We are told that in the Father's house there are many mansions, but I know there aren't enough houses in Russia."

Likewise, in *Der Gute Mensch von se-Tchouan*, three Chinese gods descend to earth. They are told that it is no longer possible to be good because men are dying of hunger; "first the pap, then comes the moral!" The gods must discover at least one good soul, one good person before they can reassure themselves and confirm that it really is possible to be honest here below. Chen-Te, a prostitute, is the only one who will give them lodgings. They pay her a thousand silver dollars which allows her to buy a tobacco shop and quit her sorry profession. But Chen-Te cannot stay respectable for long; she comes to ruin helping the innumerable poor who come to sponge off her. "How can one love when life is so dear," she says to Soun, her fiancé. On top of that, towards the end of the play, when the situation becomes far too complicated, the gods slip away, leaving vague words of encouragement. "We are only spectators" (*Wir sind nur Betrachtende*), they say, going away. The German phrase has a nuance of religious contemplation; at the same time religious comportment seems inadequate and empty. The religious man is a "confused consciousness"; he is led on by his imagination, he floats in the clouds.[1]

God seems useless; He has no connection with this game of existence. Those who believe lose themselves in the heaven of ideas. They contemplate the stars, when this is not their navel! To pass from belief to unbelief is to descend from the heaven of ideas to the world of men. Simone de Beauvoir in her *Memoirs of a Dutiful Daughter* shows this.

---

[1]B. Brecht, *Théâtre complet*, vol. III (Paris, 1955), pp. 192–96; vol. V (Paris, 1956), pp. 112–14; German edition, vol. III (Berlin, 1957), pp. 96–101; vol. VIII (Berlin, 1957), pp. 403–6.

As a believer, she loses herself in an ethereal sky, cushioned on cloud and incense. Becoming an unbeliever when she meets Sartre, she has the feeling of at last meeting someone who, in the face of reality, does not attempt to conjure it away in an idea, a word, a prefabricated system, but seizes it, teeming and sweating, in both hands. The end of the book gives the impression that Simone de Beauvoir "enters into Sartre" the same as one "enters religion," so much so that she finds herself, at last, to be in the world of men.[2]

Sartrean existentialism and Marxism meet at this point. It is sufficient to read what Sartre means by literature to see his distrust in the face of all activity of wisdom, of contemplation, in short, of humanism and religion in the sense one spontaneously gives the term:

When all is said and done, the message is a soul which is made object. A soul, and what is to be done with a soul? One contemplates it at a respectful distance. It is not customary to show one's soul in society without an imperious motive. But, with certain reserves, convention permits some individuals to put theirs into commerce, and all adults may procure it for themselves. For many people today, works of the mind are thus little straying souls which one acquires at a modest price; there is good old Montaigne's, dear La Fontaine's, and that of Jean-Jacques and of Jean-Paul and of delicious Gerard. What is called literary art is the ensemble of treatments which make them inoffensive. Tanned, refined, chemically treated, they provide their acquirers with the opportunity of devoting some moments of a life completely turned outward to the cultivation of some subjectivity. Custom guarantees it to be without risk. Montaigne's scepticism? Who can take it seriously since the author of *The Essays* got frightened when the plague ravaged Bordeaux? Or Rousseau's humanitarianism, since Jean-Jacques put his children into an orphanage? And the strange revelations of *Sylvie*, since Gerard de Nerval was mad? . . . Finally, when the internal contradictions of the life and the work have made both of them useless, when the message, in its imponderable

---

[2]S. de Beauvoir, *Mémoires d'une jeune fille rangée* (Paris, 1958), pp. 338–39 (Translation: *Memoirs of a Dutiful Daughter*).

depth, has taught us these capital truths; "that man is neither good nor bad", "that there is a great deal of suffering in human life", "that genius is only great patience", this melancholy cuisine will have achieved its purpose, and the reader, as he lays down the book, will be able to cry out with a tranquil soul, "All this is only literature."[3]

Compare this text with the affirmation of a Charles du Bos on "La vie qui est la vallée où se forment les âmes." "Life is the vale of soulmaking," according to Keats, and of the literature which is the reflection of this life of the soul, in order to measure the difference in tone. Moreover, Sartre further explains what he means by literature:

The subject of literature has always been man in the world. . . . The writer . . . would no longer seek to soar above his time and bear witness to it before eternity. . . . He would express the hopes and anger of all man, and would thereby express himself completely, that is, not as a metaphysical creature like the medieval clerk, nor a psychological animal like our classical writers, nor even as a social entity, but as a totality emerging into the world from the void and containing within it all these structures in the indissoluble entity of human condition. . . . Whether he identified himself with the good and with divine Perfection, with the Beautiful or the True, a clerk is always on the side of the oppressors. A watchdog or a jester. . . . The spiritual, moreover, always rests upon an ideology, and ideologies are freedom when they make themselves, and oppression when they are made. The writer will know that his job is not adoration of the spiritual, but rather spirtualisation. Spiritualisation, that is, *renewal*. And there is nothing else to spiritualise, nothing else to renew but this multicoloured and concrete world with its weights, its opaqueness, its zones of generalisation, and its swarms of anecdotes, and that invincible Evil which gnaw at it without ever being able to destroy it. The writer will renew it as it is, the raw, sweaty, smelly, everyday world, in order to submit it to the freedoms on the foundation of a freedom.[4]

"Destiny is the affair of men, it deals with men," as André Malraux had already said in 1926.

[3]J.-P. Sartre, *What is Literature?* (New York, 1949), pp. 33–34.
[4]*Ibid.*, pp. 156–58.

So, the soul, God, religion, all form part of these abstractions, these pseudo-absolutes which confuse consciousness and serve to justify the most oppressive tyrannies. In praising the "eternal woman" the poets confuse women and make them walk on the clouds and forget their responsibilities to society. God would be a fabrication of the same type. The fundamental realities are sociological, economic, and political. Men are hungry: "Now I know the truth of the human state of affairs," wrote Simone de Beauvoir; "two-thirds of humanity are hungry. My species is made up, in this two-thirds, by spectres, too weak to rebel, who eke out, from birth till death, a shadowy despair."[5] When faced with these facts one cannot react like the spectator gods, or with a literature which talks about "Man the Eternal."

Modern man thinks the religions have done nothing efficacious to change such a situation; sometimes they have assisted in keeping people in poverty. Simone de Beauvoir mentions in *La Force des choses* an African tribe (living along the banks of the Niger River) which is dying of hunger because its religion forbids it to eat fish. Proudhon said in 1848: "He who speaks to me about God wants either my money or my life."[6] "God is dead," cried Nietzsche. Certain moderns would add "Hurrah!"

The Church
The denial of God is often linked to indifference and distrust, if not hostility towards the Church, towards what it says and also what it does. If ecclesiastical authority orders the works of Teilhard de Chardin withdrawn from library windows, all the declarations by the same ecclesiastical authority on the liberty of scientific research will be considered as mere talk. "Words, words, words," as Hamlet said.

Albert Camus came to recognize more and more the

[5]S. de Beauvoir, *La Force des choses* (Paris, 1963), p. 682.
[6]H. de Lubac, *Proudhon et le christianisme* (Paris, 1944), p. 198; cf. *Le Drame de l'humanisme athée* (Paris, 1945).

greatness of Christ. He told a reporter for *Daghens Nyheter*, in December 1957: "I see no reason for not admitting the emotion that I feel for Christ and his teaching." It appears that Clamence, the central figure in *The Fall*, is struck by the radiance of the man Jesus. It appears that the hypocrisy and cowardice which, rightly or wrongly, he finds in our society today brings him to discover, by contrast, the sweetness of that man "who asks only one thing, that we love," and who says to the woman taken in adultery, "Go, I do not condemn you." Camus explained to a reporter of *Le Monde*: "It is true that I do not believe in God. But that does not mean that I am an atheist. I would be in agreement with Benjamin Constant in finding irreligion rather trite and vulgar."[7] Certainly he maintained right until the end, and even accentuated, his suspicion of the Catholic church. Too often, he said, the churches, in the name of the Absolute, tyrannize and oppress. The wars of religion are not so far from us.[8]

For many people, the Church speaks an abstract language with no relation to the world of concrete questions which Sartre enumerates in the texts already quoted. The "catholic" countries are very often the poorest countries, such as Spain and Latin America. The Church speaks of the hell to come, while for two-thirds of humanity life is a living hell. It introduces St. Joseph into the Canon of the Mass, while millions of men no longer believe in God. Far too often it supports conservative regimes. Is not the Vatican the last court in the world where there are breast-plated soldiers and guards dressed in frills, Henry II style? Doesn't the Palatine Guard often make one think of Offenbach's "carabiniers"? In Heinrich Böll's novel *Und Sagte kein*

[7]C. Moeller, "The Question of Hope," *Cross Currents*, VIII (1958), 183.

[8]I. Lepp, *Psychanalyse de l'athéisme moderne* (Paris, 1961), pp. 245–53; cf. Mgr. Veuillot *et al.*, *L'Athéisme, tentation du monde, réveil des chrétiens?* (Paris, 1963).

einziges wort, Bognor, the book's hero, is employed as standard-bearer to the bishopric: the word he hears most frequently is "Vorsicht," prudence! Kaiser, in his excellent book *Inside the Council,* shows that the ship, the Church, was living in a dry dock; John XXIII, wanting to gain the high seas, decided firstly to examine the rigging and the hull: this was the pre-Council phase.[9] But someone hastened to blow out the candle being used in the preparatory inspection. In all this I am citing criticism of the Roman Catholic church. Perhaps there is a more generalized alienation of the modern mind facing all the churches. Is it necessary then to introduce courses of theology and even to organize definite forms of religious life in a university? These questions have a particular pertinence in the climate I wish to discuss.

Irreligion: the Quest for Religion?

In making the above remarks to you, I have not been aware in myself of a lack of reference for God and religion. Indeed, I believe that world-wide disbelief and criticism of the Catholic church are the reverse side of a process of purification both of the Church and religion. In philosophical terms—I dare not say in philosophical jargon—this is called a dialectical moment: the principle of negativity must necessarily enter into the search for truth. This is the meaning of modern irreligion, according to excellent judges.[10]

The God who is dead is not perhaps the true God, but a convenient caricature, a "pocket God," an "echo-God," precisely that which the priest in Ingmar Bergman's recent film *Winter's Light* rejects when the echo no longer replies

[9]R. Kaiser, *Inside the Council* (London, 1963), p. 158: "Others, subconsciously falling back on the eleventh commandment, 'Thou shall not rock the boat', began a prudence campaign against any move at all towards a Council for unity."

[10]J. Lacroix, *Le Sens de l'athéisme moderne* (Tournai, Paris, 1958), p. 56; *L'Existence de Dieu* (several authors) (Tournai, Paris, 1961), pp. 13–18.

in the desired manner. The God of nature, diffused throughout the cosmos, seems dead; but this death brings up to
date an even more religious relationship between God and
man, created in his image, that is, as king of creation.
Proudhon said that *theism* was the cause of his anti-theism;
his rejection of God was made in the name of a more accurate idea of God. Too often in our times "one throws God
into the economic and social fray"; the economic situation
in France in 1848 is declared intangible, a "divine order,"
and how many apologists of this time came to accept this
order with a religious respect. Adolphé Thiers himself,
unbeliever that he was, favoured these ideas in order to
keep social peace more easily! How Proudhon knew that
God leaves man to his own resources much more than one
thinks; he knew that this so-called sacred "order" was not
an "inexplicable and mysterious providential order," but
an "easily explained result of economic circumstances."
Proudhon wished to "defatalise" the destiny of man, to
awaken him to his responsibilities to God and before God.
Thus he showed an infinitely more realistic assessment of
the true greatness of God; he separated the idea of God
from the paternalistic glue; he realized that providence is
quite a different thing to the convenient "myth" we have
made it, the same "empty providentialism" which Merleau-
Ponty was to criticize later on.

We must not, then, mourn the death of these false gods.
Religion, across the tidal wave of unbelief which is unleash-
ing itself on the world, passes through a substantial process
of cleansing. It is towards a greater God, perhaps the hidden God of the Bible (Isaiah xlv. 15), that this wave is
bearing us. This God is not the "need of the absolute," but
rather the "absolute of a need"; He is not, in any way, an
alibi releasing us from acting as responsible beings placed
in the world; He is not a nurse-maid who by daily miracles
prevents the fire from burning the child who touches it, or

the water from drowning he who ventures in without being able to swim, or the mass of political dynamite, accumulated by international tensions, blowing up in the face of anyone who goes too near. God is *not a criterion*; there is nothing "political to be learnt from Sacred Scripture." God is a *guarantee* of the ultimate metaphysical significance of all human endeavours towards truth and justice.[11]

This God is silent. "You see, heaven doesn't reply," said Camus to a friend, pointing to the blue Algerian sky filling out above the body of a young Arab run over by a bus. "The silence of God, I have thought of it all day," wrote Julien Green. And the priest in Ingmar Bergman's *Winter's Light*, when his God no longer made reply, spoke also of the silence of God, a theme which became obsessive in the last film of the trilogy, *Silence (Tysnaten)*. However, the God who is silent is often none other than the echo-God who exists only in our desires or fears. Now God "lives in an inaccessible light" (I Tim. vi. 16). The eternal temptation to idolatry reduces him continually to the dimensions of an amulet or a lucky charm. God is *"más alla,"* "above and beyond" all our images and conceptual categories. The "dark night of the soul" spoken of by St. John of the Cross is not dark through lack of light but through excess of light.[12]

The religion of *this* God has a future in the world, and in the university as well. The university, as a school of research, is in effect the ideal location for this critical study, in detail, of the phenomenon of contemporary irreligion. I do not say that the university should limit itself to this task, essential though it is. It must fill the professional ranks with doctors, engineers, lawyers, and so forth; it must promote,

[11]A. Dondeyne, *Foi chrétienne et pensée contemporaine* (Louvain, 1951), pp. 17, 32 (Translation: *Contemporary European Thought and Christian Faith*).

[12]J. Baruzi, *Saint Jean de la Croix et le problème de l'expérience mystique* (Paris, 1931).

individually and collectively, that disinterested research known as "science in the making";[13] but it must also, as the "université-universalité," cover the whole range of human knowledge to allow for the convergence of the different fields of research into the inexhaustible human reality. The religious disciplines, in this context, can make an essential contribution.

II

I should like, in this second section, to treat in detail the method through which the university, as a school, can bring about this penetrating study of the religious watermark written into the pages of profane science. In other words, I should like to describe the place of religion in formal university studies.

No Conflict

To give a place to religion in university studies, to open a faculty of religious sciences in the general programme, in no way serves to diminish the liberty of scientific research. On the contrary. The "man in white," he who, in white coat, works in the laboratory, analyzing and testing hypotheses, undoubtedly makes a strange bedfellow with the "man in black," he who, every Sabbath, dressed in a black coat, assists at service, at the temple or at the church. Often as well, the former is bored. One of the congregation attending Sunday service in the parish church was asked one day: "What are you doing here?" "I'm waiting for the finish," he replied! But, between the "man in white" and the "man in black," both of whom live in each of us, there must be something more than a gentleman's agreement or a state of cold war.

13L. de Raeymaeker, and other professors of the University of Louvain, *Truth and Freedom*, coll. Duquesnes Studies, Philosophical series, vol. V (Pittsburgh, 1954), p. 11.

If one were to represent the relations between religion and the other university disciplines in the manner of the territory which belongs respectively to the "man in black" and the "man in white," border incidents would be inevitable. What is more, the "man in white," the scientist, would be changing the borders, always to the advantage of science. If one were to divide, by means of a straight line, the separate fields of medical science and religious science, the walls of separation would always go in the same direction: areas which one believed to be "strictly religious," inviolable to medical science, will now be revealed as accessible to it. Advances in labotomy, which can turn a scrupulous person obsessed with the idea of suicide into an almost "happy-go-lucky" person making the most of life, demand prudence when it is a question of determining just what is a human personality. In the same way, truth serums make us consider the true concept of human liberty: we must not identify it with physico-chemical conditions which can be treated medically. Aldous Huxley's *Brave New World* is as relevant as ever.

In other words, we must abandon any false representation. Otherwise, the area "reserved" for God, the cleared ground of religious manoeuvre—if such a familiar expression is permissible—will contract dangerously. In the same way as does the itchy skin in Honoré de Balzac's famous novel, the religious field will shrivel up. In the end, as the saying goes, God will be "with his back to the wall." We must reject this vision of things. Religion does not live on the fringe of obscurity, in the shadow that science creates around itself. One of the characters in *Les Thibault*, a novel by Roger Martin du Gard, makes this mistake. Abbé Vécard, speaking with Antoine Thibault, an atheistic doctor, afirms that science does not explain everything; it is in this fringe of obscurity that one places God. But God is not "localised" in this way in the fissures of scientific determinism, in the lacuna of scientific explanation: today's gaps will be filled tomorrow, by science herself.

We must abandon the idea of an empire of human knowledge subdivided into nations, provinces, and districts. For example, the doctor who is treating, with physiological medication, a person with moral scruples or a sexual obsession affects not just one aspect of his patient, a type of superficial skin, but the whole, complete man. The psychologist who treats the same patient affects him also in his entirety, as does the sociologist and the economist. Our patient is all this together, at one and the same time. It is not because the psychologist treats the moral scruples by coming to grips with the "conscience" that the role of the doctor loses any of its importance. Moreover, it is not because the priest helps the sexually obsessed person with spiritual means that the doctor's work on the same patient will lose one iota of its importance. The anointing of the sick does not preclude the need for medical care, for the Church orders a medical examination, at the same time proceeding with the ceremonies of exorcism. In the person of the Jesuit, Paneloux, in Camus' *The Plague*, who resigns himself to the will of God and refuses to be treated when struck by the plague, we have a caricature of true obedience to the will of God.

To be sure, theologians will always have a tendency to say that their approach to man is, in the long run, the only one which really counts. But they are wrong, as equally wrong as those who state that the only true approach to man is medical, sociological, or biological. Specialization, even though it be theological, always runs the same risk: that of enmeshing itself in one point of view in such a way that everything tends to start from this point only. It is what the philosopher, A. N. Whitehead, called the fallacy of misplaced concreteness. We think that the crab moves strangely because he doesn't walk as we do; but the crab undoubtedly thinks in turn that men are animals with a strange way of moving!

I have just borrowed an example from religion. I did so on purpose. From the aspect of university studies, religion is *one* of the global approaches, one of the perspectives of reality. Undoubtedly this perspective is all-embracing. Undoubtedly again—I shall return to this point—religious analysis, from its point of view, answers an *ultimate* question on the sense of life. But the greater importance of this point of view detracts in no way from the autonomy and the necessity of other fields of research. Man *is* an ensemble as fully, in his very depths, as the political animal of Aristotle, the economic man of Marxism, the gentleman or honest man in English or French humanism. He is also religious man, the "man in black" who goes to the temple, even if he is bored and the only thing he remembers from the sermon on sin is that "the preacher was rather against it. . . ." These points of view which do not overlap nevertheless do not oppose each other. It is not by an academic proportioning nor by an equilibrium achieved in compromise that the marriage between the "man in black" and the "man in white" will succeed. In a sense, man is completely man in white, scientist, and completely man in black, religious man. He is the point of convergence of all these perspectives, each one adequate in its aim, each one limited in its point of view. It is not the static abstract synthesis of these truths but their dynamic complementariness which constitutes man.

It is *not in the object* itself that the division of zones is situated, but in *the point of view* starting from which each perspective is taken, the starting place from which the observer cuts out, in the totality of reality, the profiles which Husserl calls *Abschattungen*. In other words, if I look at a face, I shall never be able to see the nape of the neck at the same time, and inversely, but my perspective of this man's face is achieved globally. It is the whole man I grasp, with a global vision, when I look upon him. I know everything about this man and at the same time I have a particular viewpoint. No one can have at the same time consciousness and knowledge of all the perspectives whose least object is susceptible. But each viewpoint, each profile is complete in its aim though it is incomplete according to its point of observation.

When Marxists criticized the "petit-bourgeois" infra-structure of the characters in *Doctor Zhivago* written by Pasternak, they were emphasizing an authentic aspect of the book. Certainly the characters are not just their economic and social unbringing; they are also shaped by this upbringing and they are it totally. The humanistic approach of Pasternack's work takes away nothing from the pertinence and utility of the criticism made of the economic foundations of the same characters.

In other words, the scientific point of view is autonomous. It touches all reality and not just a superficial part of it. The statement of Jean Rostand's, that "from the scientific point of view, there is only a difference in degree of complexity between the brain of Mozart and the brain of a fly," is true provided we do not neglect the first few words "from the scientific point of view." If one were to forget this distinction, if one were to believe, theoretically or practically, that the necessarily descriptive aspect of biological science is the only one of value, one would pass from perfectly legitimate methodological "materialism," which consists in explaining, for example, psychology by physiology as did the doctor, to philosophical materialism, which reduces the superior to the inferior, the psychological to the physiological, the cultural to the economic.

"Is science autonomous?" asks Professor Ladrière. Yes and no is his answer, depending on the sense of the word autonomous.

The term "autonomy" may be understood in two different senses. Taken in the extreme sense, autonomy would mean that a system is totally self-contained or closed. In a wider sense,

the autonomy of a science means that this science has a con-
sistency of its own. It should be clear that the sciences cannot
be considered to be totally closed with respect to one another.
They have mutual relationships, and these relationships can
affect them rather profoundly, not only because sciences may be
able to enrich one another through their results or methods,
but also because they study *different aspects of one and the
same reality.*[14]

And, a little further on, he explains:

Every type of human experience is characterized by an evidence
of its own. For instance, there is an evidence proper to sense
perception, another proper to esthetic perception, a third proper
to emotion, and so forth. This amounts to saying that the characteristic object of each of these types of experience has its own
way of expressing itself upon the mind to which it is presented.
For example, we do not live an emotion of fear in the same
way as the esthetic emotion which is aroused by the sight of a
beautiful monument. . . . Each of these types of evidence is
connected with what we may call a fundamental attitude. The
term "attitude", of course, must not be taken here in the psychological sense. There is no question here of this or that type
of reaction to a given situation, but of an innate mode of the
mind. In speaking of a *fundamental* attitude we want to indicate
that there is question here of a mode which is prior to the
external attitude whose description can be given by methods of
objective psychology. . . . The fundamental attitude is a way of
viewing reality, a way of approaching the objects which throng
the universe in which we live. Accordingly, several different
fundamental attitudes are possible with respect to the same
reality.[15]

In physics, for example, two aspects of this type of "evidence" are followed: experience and theory, a dualism
which is essential. The mathematical structure of the world
is not sought after for its own sake, but through it we gain
a certain view of the world. "And this world, in final analysis, is the same world as was given to us in naive experience,
except that it has been stripped of the characteristics proper

[14]*Ibid.*, p. 93.   [15]*Ibid.*, p. 94.

to it in that level and is grasped according to the type of intelligibility that is supplied by mathematical objects."

Moreover, theology has its own fundamental attitude and type of evidence:

In the totality of human knowledge, theology occupies a very special place. The reason is that theological attempts of explanation are not directed towards the world given in our naive experience, but rather towards a reality which has become accessible to us only by means of revelation. This Revelation is within our reach only through the written text of a book which, for the believer, is directly inspired by God and therefore represents His word, and through the tradition of a religious society which, for the believer, was instituted by God and presents itself as the guardian of His word. . . . Theology is a methodical effort of man's reason which applies itself with all the resources at its disposal, including those supplied by philosophy, to the interpretation of the data of this Revelation. It is in this Revelation that theology finds, at the same time, its foundations and its limits. Its *foundation*, because the whole work of theology consists in faithfulness to the data of Revelation. . . . Theology finds its *limits* also in the interpretation of the data of Revelation: these data surpass the capacities of reason. . . . Consequently the experience of Faith is radically different from both the philosophical and the scientific attitudes and does not put forward a claim to substitute itself for them. Undoubtedly, theology which, as it were, systematically renders this experience of faith explicit on the level of discourse, will be induced to project its light upon the realms of reality in which the physical sciences are interested. Yet, in doing so, theology remains in its own order. It neither offers these sciences a new system of evidences nor imposes upon them a regulating principle to which they would have to submit.[16]

I cannot emphasize sufficiently the last lines, for they are the basis of the following affirmation, even more essential to our subject:

For the believer, scientific research is not merely accepted in the name of a principle of intellectual tolerance, but also because it

[16]*Ibid.*, pp. 99–100.

possesses a positive value which fully justifies the efforts which he consecrates to it when he engages in this research. . . . The truth accessible to science is part of the whole truth, and it is man's function to discover as much as possible of the truth, by using the means God has placed at his disposal for this purpose. Each time it is possible to use reason to perform a work of research, it must be used for it. For the believer, this application of reason to research is not an operation resulting from a curiosity which could, perhaps, be in vain. On the contrary, for him, research assumes the appearance of a work that praises God. And he knows that he will be able to make his research a genuine work of praise if, and only if, he conforms scrupulously to the requirements of research.[17]

"It is good to offer science to God," said Etienne Gilson, "yet there must *be* a science, otherwise we offer nothing at all!"[18] Thus, "without being totally closed, positive science is autonomous in the sense that it is constituted in the light of its own principles."[19]

In the same way, no more than there are two mathematics, one Christian and one otherwise, there are not two types of history. There is only one, the *good*, according to the type of evidence and the criteria peculiar to historical research. "The story is told of a monk working in a storehouse of archives who one day declared, so the story goes, that if he were to discover any document prejudicial to the Catholic Church he would not hesitate to destroy it and thus forestall its use as an argument against his faith."[20] Without going as far as that, how many Christian historians do not hesitate to choose their documents in such a way as to present only an "edifying," apologetic image of the Church's history!

It is time to conclude this section with a more general

[17]*Ibid.*, p. 101.
[18]Quoted in Y. Congar, *Jalons pour une théologie du laïcat*, coll. Unam Sanctam, vol. XXIII (Paris, 1953), p. 548. "La piété ne dispense jamais de la technique."
[19]De Raeymaeker *et al.*, *Truth and Freedom*, p. 101.
[20]*Ibid.*, p. 79.

thought. It is taken from a talk by Cardinal Mercier, founder and first president of the Institut supérieur de philosophie at the Catholic University of Louvain. In an address given at the university on December 8, 1907, he said:

Most certainly, there are times when neutrality is imperative— namely when one is engaged in scientific research. The problems of physics, chemistry, or biology, those of history or social economy should not be approached with the preconceived notion of finding in them a confirmation of one's religious beliefs. . . . To consider a science from another angle than the one which is offered by its formal objects, to approach the consideration of this object with an attention divided between this object and a task belonging to apologetics, such an attitude is a misconception of the essence itself of scientific speculation and goes directly against the very progress which the man of research is supposed to pursue. . . . The Catholic scholar is *certain* of the truth of the faith. . . .

Accordingly, he is certain, too, unshakeably certain, that no new discovery will ever contradict the object of his belief. As a result, the Christian scholar who would be perturbed about the possible future development of science, would be lacking either in Faith or in scientific spirit, or in both.[21]

No False Harmonization

Although there cannot be conflicts between religion and science in the context of university disciplines, we must not seek a false reconciliation between these two divisions. It was held for a long time, quite wrongly, that Darwinism is

[21]*Ibid.*, pp. 16–17. On page 15 is a commentary by de Raeymaeker: "For this reason also, as a firm believer in his faith, he considered that the best service which researchers could render to religious truth in the realm of science was to surrender themselves to their research with all their power, without any restrictive fear, without any prejudice, without any thought other than that of bringing their research to a successful conclusion in the domain in which it was conducted. Therefore also, they should have no concern about apologetics, for even a preoccupation of this order is able to obscure their mind in their work, turn it away from the intended aim and thus make them miss the discovery of a truth."

opposed to the religious truths in the book of Genesis. In answer to this contention people have tried to find a harmony, a sort of parallelism between the geological ages of science and the six "days" of Genesis! An empty and futile labour: Genesis teaches quite a different truth which leaves intact, in order, the hypothesis of evolution.

It would be false to believe that the dream of a harmony between religion and science has totally disappeared. Many readers still imagine that Jean Rostand denied the truth of religious values in the name of biological science, the field in which he was an expert. Now there is no connection between Rostand's agnosticism and his work as a biologist. His conviction as to the uncertainty of the significance of religion was not based on his scientific research. Inversely, others think that the conflict between science and religion being a thing of the past, science is moving closer to religion, is orienting itself in that direction. When Lecomte du Nouy explains, in *L'Avenir de l'esprit*, that in the appearance of the first molecule of protein—it is a question here of living matter—everything happens as if a trickster intervened to falsify the calculation of probability, which, left to itself would not yet have allowed the appearance of life, he is undoubtedly stating a scientific fact. But if one said that this "trickster," orienting evolution in the sense of a "telefinality" (or finality of ensembles), allows one to proceed to the idea of God, one would fall into a harmony as disastrous as that between the geological ages and the six "days" of creation. One would be just as gravely mistaken in interpreting the hypotheses of Père Teilhard de Chardin on the "omega point," the divine pole, evolution towards the "nowhere," as a scientific affirmation, or a scientific proof, of the existence of God. Père Teilhard, whom I had the pleasure of meeting, never thought this. He wished to add to the strictly biological perspective another perspective, starting from the hypothesis of a personalizing principle. He

did not give in to false harmonization, that is, to the temptation of a gradual passage from the biological vision to the
religious vision. Moreover, some of his writings, especially
The Phenomenon of Man, are a little ambiguous; too many
readers imagine, after the long night of a science which
denied religion, the dawn of a science which would sub-
stantiate or at least make room for religion!

Now there is not, and cannot be, any scientific proof of
the existence of God. It would be just as fatal to interpret
Jean Rostand in the sense of an irreligious materialism as to
explain Teilhard in the sense of a "physics of the spirit."
Here again is a complementariness of approaches, of perspectives on the one reality which will always escape defini-
tive formulation.[22]

Scientific Study of Religion

We must go even further. In the context of the university,
religion must be studied in a strictly scientific manner, con-
forming to critical methods. This does not mean that theology must submit itself to the criterion of that mathematical
measurement which is proper to the physical sciences.
Theology has its own method, as we have said.[23] It has a
particular perspective, the spirit of which it must always
strive to retain. The original, specific character of the religious method cannot be reduced, when it is understood
properly, to the methods of economic or political science.
However, Revelation, which is at the core of the Christian
religion, comes to us across the pages of history; this history is linked up with these texts; the texts themselves
belong to quite varied literary forms, as form-criticism
(*Formgeschichte*) emphasizes; finally, religious language
uses allegories, parables, symbols, and myths. The study of

[22]The best book on Teilhard, from the point of view of religion is
H. de Lubac, *La Pensée religieuse de Teilhard de Chardin* (Paris, 1962).
[23]De Raeymaeker *et al.*, *Truth and Freedom*, p. 99. Cf. *supra*.

the Christian religious subjects implies then, as well, an analysis of the religious reality beginning with the corresponding disciplines of history and philosophy. It is not a question of subjecting religion to the "masters of suspicion," as Paul Ricoeur calls Marx, Nietzsche, and Freud,[24] but of applying to the religious reality all the perspectives of approach by which it presents itself to us.

In the first place, historical research has an essential role. God, by the Incarnation, entered into history; thus there exists a "sacred history." *Sacred* history certainly, and one must not lose sight of this aspect, but *history* as well, for it does not unfold in an empyrean abstract, "nowhere" and "at no particular time," but is united organically to the fibre of the history of the Mediterranean Near East. The historical study of the destiny of the Fertile Crescent stretching from Mesopotamia to Egypt outlines the complexity of cultural and religious traditions at the same time as it shows the original aspect of Jewish monotheism and the awaited Messiah. These golden threads seem blended to an extremely primitive fabric; thus their originality stands out better. Jewish monotheism is not a meteorite dropped from another planet, but the patient discovery of a greater and more universal God by a people whose prophets could scarcely turn them away from idolatory. And we, we are this people. We must pursue the pious malefactors who, under pretext of apologetics, falsify texts. The Bible is not "edifying," still less is it moralizing. Never, for example, does it show us visibly the just being rewarded, but speaks rather of Job and Jeremiah, of Jesus, the suffering just; biblical personalities such as David and Solomon did not have time to pose for the stained-glass window painters. The history into which biblical revelation plunges us is earthy and bloody, full of love but also ugliness. Happily,

---

[24]Paul Ricoeur explained this in 1961 in his lectures at the Chaire Cardinal Mercier, in Louvain, on "Religion et reflexion critique."

indeed! for this is our history which the prophetic message enlightens with a ray of hope.

In the second place, phenomonology and philosophy must be used in analyzing religion. We must reflect critically on the symbols and religious myths used in the Bible and Christian preaching. Three remarks will clarify this point, which is especially important in the present situation. First, to speak of symbol and myth is not to relegate religion to the ranks of the fables destined to console an infantile humanity. To play with a doll and to believe in fairies at the age of forty "is not to be serious"; it can be diverting but only at the price of fleeing reality. We know that Levy-Bruhl criticized the "pre-logical" thought of the ancients; if this thought is only *pre*-logical, it must hasten to bypass this state of prolonged infancy to reach an adult age of logical knowledge. Myth, *mythos*, here is radically opposed to *logos*, the symbolic logical word.

Now, symbol and myth are quite different things as Professor Levy-Strauss shows. Thus neither in the orphic myth of the origin of evil, born from the exile of the soul in its prison, the body (sema-soma, the word-play prison-body, becomes commonplace in orphism and is refound in the myth of the cave in Plato's *Republic*), nor in Genesis where we have the serpent and the tree of knowledge of good and evil, are there any naïve fables, but rather forms of thought; "still less are they opposed to the simple logical thought which completes them. In fact, all expression of mysterious truths cannot abandon, purely and simply, mythical thought and its forms of spontaneous expression, even if it must criticize them."[25] Thus the symbolism of the fruit eaten by man and of the tempting serpent signifies a complex truth that no purely philosophical or conceptual formulation can ever adequately express. On the one hand, the fruit of the tree of knowledge shows that evil appears in the world not

[25]L. Bouyer, *Dictionnaire théologique* (Paris, 1963), p. 453.

by virtue of an Oedipean fatality, but by the free choice of man, that which Kant called the malice of the will. On the other hand, the presence of the serpent signifies that man enters into a world where evil already exists; this truth is as evident as the first but when reflected upon too systematically at the philosophical level it leads to one or the other form of dualist gnosticism, dividing the universe into separate zones of malicious darkness and divine light. These two symbols, taken together, point to an essential truth: that man is entirely free and also that he enters a world where evil already exists.[26]

There is then an evidence peculiar to symbol and myth. Phenomenology unveils it, showing the specific character of this perspective of the human reality. In other words, man is not firstly a child, a primitive person with "fabulous" thought, then a philosopher, and finally a scientist. The triple division of August Comte is false if one places it in a chronological perspective, where temporal succession is made a scale of value, implying that that which came "before" is less valuable than that which comes "after." We must turn this triple division of Comte around and see that each man is, at the same time, this threefold approach to human reality. I have already said, but I wish to repeat, even at the risk of being tiresome that man simultaneously engages in exact scientific research, philosophical reflection, and the search for the meaning of life with the help of religious symbolism. To suppress symbolic thought, or reduce it, on the pretext of transcending infantilism, to scientific or philosophical elements of which it would be only a projection, is to mutilate man. Man needs the sacred. Deprived of it, he wanders aimlessly into impersonal cities, and he seeks in the "ersatz," for example in the sexuality rife in big cities, a type of substitute for the sacred. This mutila-

[26]P. Ricoeur, *Finitude et culpabilité*, vol. II, *La Symbolique du mal* (Paris, 1960), pp. 218–61.

tion has been tried many times, not only in totalitarian regimes but also in democratic ones when they sell out to a higher bidder—the sociological and economic conditioning of man. Here one thinks again of Aldous Huxley's prophetic book, *Brave New World*, where the absence of any symbolic dimension, or its travesty, inspires a grim irony.

Furthermore, there are different types of symbols. The "fables" which Bergson analyzes in the enclosed, sociological religion which is marked by social constraint are the projection of man's fear in the face of death. Void society (and the individuals which form it) manages in some way to find an antidote for death: invented fables, born from fear and produced by the biological, egoistical, and individual "will to survive." "We do not believe, Father, we fear," said an Eskimo to a missionary who was questioning him about his religion.[27]

If, then, there are some symbols which cannot stand up to critical reflection, which reveal themselves, for example, as the sublimation of the "sur-moi," there are others which are more profoundly understood by this analysis. I believe that "the Bible constantly uses myth," but gives it "an altogether new, profound, and pure content."[28] The above outline of the symbol of the fruit and the serpent seems to be quite adequate in this regard.

Finally, we must transcend the naïve comprehension by which myths are received and understood. We must not project or spread the story of the Fall of Adam into a verifiable space and time. In other words, despite the great complexity of the subject, we must "demythologise" (*Entmythologisieren*) the myths. But inversely, it would be quite wrong to "demythise" (*Entmythisieren*), for example, by reducing the Genesis narrative to a simple non-temporal

[27]H. Bergson, *Les Deux Sources de la morale et de la religion* (Paris, 1937).
[28]Bouyer, *Dictionnaire théologique*, p. 453.

allegory, to a moral lesson taught to children in metaphor, but failing to learn anything of the real history of humanity and its present condition.[29] In these narratives there is something that cannot be reduced to a simple *logos* or timeless discourse, for they have an aim which surpasses the purely conceptual understanding. The Genesis narrative is not history because it is more than history; it affirms the reality of a fundamental event constituting a sinful state for all humanity. The prophetic accusation against evil is so permanent, so radical that it already suggests a mysterious origin, and the Genesis narrative clarifies for us this secret cause.[30]

It is no longer possible to cling to the "first naivety" of the child who does not distinguish between *Alice in Wonderland* and the story of the first man in the Garden of Eden. We must criticize symbol and myth. But this criticism does not lead to the demystification of the adult in a profane world, but to what Paul Ricoeur calls the "second naivety." "The symbol adds something to thought," he said, not beyond itself in the disillusionment of an abstract *logos*, but in its very depths, in rediscovered naivety, a gift of wonder, of reflection, a sense of the sacred—the "awe" spoken of by Newman, the "numinous" of Rudolph Otto— without which no man can live.[31] "After all, truth is perhaps sad," said Renan. Criticism had destroyed the poetic images

[29]In the French translation of R. Bultmann, *L'Interprétation du Nouveau Testament* (Paris, 1955), this distinction between "démythologiser" and "démythiser" is neglected! Cf. J. A. T. Robinson, *Honest to God* (SCM Paperback, London, 1963), and M. Ramsey, *Image Old and New* (London, 1963).

[30]Bultmann makes a distinction between *Historisch* (the story as written in the books of annalists) and *Geschichtlich* (the event which is claiming of the man an *Existenzielle Entschluss*). It is *not* in this sense that I am speaking here, of a myth which is "more than a story." Cf. L. Malevez, *Le Message chrétien et le mythe* (Bruxelles, Paris, 1954), and R. Marle, *Bultmann et l'interprétation du Nouveau Testament*, coll. Théologie, vol. 33 (Paris, 1956).

[31]Ricoeur, *La Symbolique du mal*, pp. 323–32.

of his Christian infancy. These were only images. But the second naivety, reflection on the symbol, has no connection with a return to the mists of childhood. Christianity is not nostalgia for a paradise lost, a return home, but a capacity to assume the human reality, including the "sad truths" spoken of by Renan. The "truth" which communicates to us the myth of the Fall, beyond this reflection, is not a convenient and chilly refuge; it is entirely composed of responsibility and liberty, in a world where obstacles cannot be conjured away. This truth is the very opposite of a mystification.

A short illustration will conclude this third series of reflections. When one looks over Paris from the top of the Eiffel Tower it can be seen that the city has grown up around the cathedral of Notre-Dame. French roads are measured to start from the Cathedral square. We are in a world where the sacred can still be discerned quite easily in the very stones of a city. How many other European cities have been built around a monastic church or cathedral! But, on the contrary, when one surveys New York from the top of the Empire State Building, one imagines oneself to be in a city created by man for the glory of man. St. Patrick's Cathedral, as big as Notre-Dame, is found only with difficulty, for it is hidden, almost crushed, by the massive Rockefeller Center. One has the feeling of being in a world of concrete and steel, functional, scientific, but also "demystified" and radically profane. But this is only an appearance. The first naivety is soon succeeded by a second naivety which rediscovers, together with the contribution of science and thanks to it, a more profound aspect of man's world where the sacred also exists. New York is sprinkled with churches—often full of worshippers. From the Prudential Building in Chicago the Chicago Basilica can be seen. This is a Methodist house of prayer; it is situated on the ground floor of a skyscraper office block. Alongside the express, semi-direct and on all floors elevators which go up and return ceaselessly, there is this place of recollection where men and women pray. Humanity is, at one and the same time, the crowd which is taken up by these elevators and this community which prays. Man in white, man in black. . . .

Contribution of Religion to the Other University Disciplines
I should like to end this second section by proposing several thoughts on what a faculty of theology or religious sciences can *irreplaceably* bring to other university studies. First, theology does not impose edicts upon the other sciences which limit their freedom to work. It was not in this sense that philosophy was formerly spoken of as the "servant of theology" (*ancilla theologiae*). "As soon as scientific research would be directed by other principles of science, there would no longer be science. . . . Once again, this law is an internal law of science," writes Professor Ladrière.[32] Thus, the presence of religious faculties in a university cannot mean, either theoretically or practically, a clericalization of thought and research.

If it is true, from the strictly scientific point of view, that the religious perspective adds to the philosophical, cultural, economic, social, and other perspectives of man, it follows that the light which religion throws is of particular importance with regard to its own point of view, that is to say, the questions which it poses on the *ultimate* meaning of the human adventure. History is drama for the thoughtful man, tragedy for the sensitive. If this history, rife with murder and violence, ends in oblivion, the fact that man may live on earth for another 60,000 years as P. Blanchard thought or for millions of years no longer has any importance in the eyes of the spirit. The last man in a decaying physical world, be he demi-urge or demi-god, would still be the last

[32]De Raeymaeker *et al.*, *Truth and Freedom*, p. 100.

man. He would ask himself what is the meaning of this life. If its purpose were not the "liberation of an immortal psyche" or better, the recapitulation of humanity in justice and love, there would be no meaning at all, a "non-sense."[33] The human goal, therefore, is justice and love: justice among men, by every effort of civilization, by the construction of a united world where riches are more equitably distributed, justice possible for the first time for all men and between all men, because for the first time each can act upon all and can influence each other;[34] and human love in solidarity, friendship, fraternal and filial affection, as well as in the loving encounter of man and woman, an encounter at the spiritual level but also at the sensible and physical level, becoming a language, a word.

Does all this make sense when contrasted with the obsolescence of the universe in the kingdom of God spoken of by the prophets? Will the end of time be marked by the great apocalyptic upheaval? Does the physical expression of the love between a man and a woman have a religious meaning, not despite of but because of its physical nature? Teilhard de Chardin had posed this question in 1917 in a series of letters to Maurice Blondel. For me, he said in substance, the major problem is to know if what nine-tenths of humanity accomplish during nine-tenths of their lives, working in the transient world as lawyer, engineer, doctor, farmer, tradesman, and so forth, has any meaning in relation to the coming of the kingdom of God.[35] This question, the meaning of secular, was also the object of a university study group at the Oecumenical Institute at Bossey, Switzerland, in 1962. The world is waiting for the council to state

[33]R. Grousset, *Bilan de l'hisoire* (Paris, 1949), chapter entitled "Sur une pensée de Pascal."

[34]T. Mende, *Entre la peur et l'espoir* (Paris, 1958); *Regards sur l'histoire de demain* (Paris, 1954).

[35]Cf. *Archives de philosophie*, nos. 1–2 (1961). In this sense, D. Bonhoeffer spoke of "Christianity without religion." He found God in the midst of man's agony.

several simple principles in which human work will find itself assumed, integrated, and justified religiously, without disappearing under, dare we say short-circuited by, the overriding current of religious experience! In this matter modern man no longer wants a pseudo-mystical or clerical sleight-of-hand. The schema XVII of the Vatican Council on "The Church in the Modern World" will deal with this very important question.

Religion, by its presence in the field of university studies, can be the proof of the prime importance of this interrogation which *engulfs* all other questions. Without denying the legitimacy or the necessity of other scientific perspectives, it suggests an ultimate meaning embracing all methods of research at the same time. The absence of this religious science would mean running the risk of losing the view of the ensemble, what we have already called the "université-universalité" of human knowledge; it would lead to an even more regrettable fissure between the different specialist fields.

Religion does not step in here to fill the gaps in other branches of knowledge but to bring fresh light, a new hypothesis on the same facts. Without taking away from the autonomy of specialized research or from man's responsibility in the universe where he must build a human world, religious research can enlighten with a more profound, universal clarity this ensemble of facts. For believers, this meaning is a truth; for others, unbelievers or agnostics, it at least represents a hypothesis worthy of consideration.

Finally, theological research must, in some way, present God, "the most present absence there is," as Charles du Bos admirably expresses it in his excellent book *What Is Literature?* For religion must give a profound meaning not only to human endeavour, but also to the *"insolubilia,"* those irreducible conflicts, those existential or inevitable equations of the human state: we are situated in a place and a contingent space; we are destined to death (*Zum Tode* said Heidegerr). Suffering, loneliness, death, what Gabriel Marcel calls the "stridencies" of life, and which usually produce cacophony rather than a symphony, cannot be resolved by purely human endeavour. Chen-Te, in *Der Gute Mensch von Se-Tchouan*, gave 200 dollars to an aged family which had just been ruined; thus she put off indefinitely her marriage to Soun, a good for nothing aviator. She is sacrificed to justice and solidarity. However, she wants to get married to Soun. When, under the tree, he caresses her face, she is inexplicably happy. But she must leave him. From the scientific point of view, this suffering is undoubtedly the statistically inevitable loss in a world founded on the law of averages. But this explains nothing to her. Why is it she who today suffers this inevitable loss? She and not someone else? The problem cannot be settled decisively either by economics or sociology. A transcendence is indicated which does not suppress the pertinence of the "secular" viewpoint but embraces it in a new dimension. So for non-believers Don Quixote remains the most Castillian of heroes at the same time as he is the most universal proof of the unwearying, *human* restlessness. The Christian characteristic which Cervantes finally lets us see—that this "chivalry" is nothing compared to the other, the heavenly—certainly deepens the profane aspect but does not destroy it. The image of man in modern European literature has, in the same way, a complex, existential meaning; it has a meaning in itself, but it also bears, in filigree, a more profound religious significance. This is at least a possible hypothesis.

Man is shown as being autonomous, contingent, culpable. It is not necessary to insist greatly on autonomy, unless to recall that it concerns everyone, for each person has a responsibility to himself and to others. Moreover, this liberty, which is also a concrete responsibility, must commit itself.

It is easy to have clean hands when one keeps them out of everything. It is easy to say "no," said Creon to Anouilh's Antigone, under pretext of not being able to have everything immediately as when one was a child; but life must continue despite that because someone must captain the ship and be obliged at certain moments to "help himself." "Kantianism has pure hands," said Péguy, "because it has no hands."[36]

The same man is also a contingency. St. Gregory spoke of life as a *quaedam prolixitas mortis,* as a sort of display, of anticipation of death within life itself. Curiously, those who today preach the "best sermons" on death are no longer the Christian writers but such as Camus, Simone de Beauvoir, Sartre, Bataille, all witnesses to the vanity of the world. They describe physical death, the living death too, which characterizes our "social relationships" as much as our vaunted self-knowledge. Jeanine, a woman in the novel *The Adulterous Woman* by Camus, discovers one night that if she could overcome her dread of dying she would be happy, but she overcomes nothing at all and "she was going to die without being set free." In the same way the loss of faith in Simone de Beauvoir was accompanied by a dread of personal death which caused her, one afternoon when she was alone in her parents' study, to "scream and scratch the red moquette" and wonder "what other people did when their end was approaching."

Death anticipates itself, in a sense, in our very life. We are dead men reprieved, not only because every morning brings us nearer the final term, but still more because we are not sure of really existing. What are we? Are we at least something? Among the masks that the interior comedy continually lays over our incoherent abyss of desire and

[36]J. Anouilh, *Antigone* (Paris, 1943); the same problem is dealt with in J.-P. Sartre, *Les Mains sales* (Paris, 1948), and in M. Merleau-Ponty, *Humanisme et terreur* (Paris, 1953).

fear, which is the true one? Alain Guimez, in *Le Planeta-rium* by Nathalie Sarraute, does not know who he is. He thinks he is an artist, for he is researching Roman art, and he builds an essential part of his life around a woman's recognition of the fact of his being an artist, a woman who has the reputation of being an artist herself. But what is this Germaine Lemaître? Is she not a caricature of the artist? In the same way, the French heroine of the film *Hiroshima mon amour* does not know who she is. Her name is "Nevers" as her Japanese lover's name is "Hiroshima," and she is so mixed up with the events of the war, so emptied of her personal substance, that she no longer exists, literally: she is nothing more now than a girl in love, whose love has been brutally broken by war; she is nothing more than "the impossibility of loving." At the moment when she loves her Japanese friend, she lives this love as though it had already been lived, at Nevers in France, as though it is already dead, dead at the very heart of apparent life.

At the same time the contingency of social relations is suggested. The life of society is comedy, parallel mono-logues, and no real understanding ever occurs. The theme is not new, but in the theatre of Adamov, Pirandello, Diego, Fabbri, Ionesco, it takes on a burlesque and tragic form. Thus in *The Bald Prima Donna* by Ionesco, there is neither a singer nor a bald woman, but a series of characters who think they know each other, who recognize each other, but who are lost in a maze. Monsieur and Madame Martin, who in the eyes of the spectator are husband and wife, seem to have forgotten the fact, and only by degrees do they observe that as they live in the same town, the same street, the same house, the same floor, and finally the same room they must be husband and wife. The little girl, who has one black eye and one red, is apparently the proof of this fact although the parents do not know the same child; for the girl of Monsieur Martin it is the left eye which is red, while for the girl of Madame Martin it is the right eye which is red! There is a mistake over the person, for *à chacun sa vérité*. Similarly in Robbe-Grillet's *L'Année dernière à Marienbad*, the characters who "meet" do not know whether they have really seen each other or recognize each other, if they really talked to each other last year! Where shall we find the resources to overcome the feeling of interior emptiness, of the *vacio*, of the *insustancialidád*, of the metaphysical insubstantiality of personal life and life in society, which haunted Unamuno? *La vida es sueño*, life is a dream. Calderon and Shakespeare said it long ago, but it is always true, truer than ever, in modern literature.

These same modern characters know themselves to be guilty. Not only has the sense of the responsibility of each for all made its entry into the universe of the novel, even to the point of dethroning concern for "interior" life for the sake of a generous but simplist social exteriority, but the feeling of guilt has grown out of it. Beyond the dialectics of "master and slave" central to Marxism, was revealed the dialectic of the "judge and the judged." Clamence in *The Fall* by Camus, Temple Drake in Faulkner's *Requiem for a Nun*, Frantz von Gerlach in Sartre's *Les Séquestrés d'Altona*, are all three haunted by a sense of guilt, all the more devastating because accompanied by the certitude that there is no transcendent judge, no heavenly father, who, while proclaiming law and judgment, can restore life and reconcile. Frantz von Gerlach, for example, objects to his father as judge and requires him to judge him.

Writers like Thomas Mann, James Joyce, T. S. Eliot, Faulkner, Kafka, throw a deep light on this situation by revealing the break in the bond of paternity which aims beyond the human level to the paternity of God. Kafka made this the centre of his universe, and Joyce wove it into the central idea of his books where man is ceaselessly in search of himself and others. Thus Daedalus, the new Telemachus, in *Ulysses*, is looking for his father, in order to find out what he himself is, the son of Bloom or a bastard, in order to find out if he is and what he is. Bloom, on the other hand, the new Ulysses, is looking for his son; he is also seeking to find again the "bond of love" with his wife Molly, the new Penelope of the atomic age. But neither Daedalus nor Bloom will ever know whether they have found each other, whether even they have ever been anything more than shadows. If they wander thus in an odyssey which never reaches the point of return, it is because, somewhere, in immemorial time, but leaving an impression on the present in depth, a link has been broken deliberately, that of the engendering of the son by the father, that of the filiation, with its origin in love which has joined two beings. This ontological break can be felt in the page of onomatopeia with which Joyce opens the "vicio-cyclous-monster" of *Finnegans Wake*. This cascade of sounds, wherein allusions to more than twenty-six world languages are heard in puns and allusions, is devoid of meaning; it makes one feel chaos, not the chaos over which brooded the Spirit of God, making it fruitful, giving it form, bringing to birth, life, love, and the knowledge of love, but the chaos which is created by man, proceeding from the rupture of the bond of paternity. The world of art remains the only outlet for man. But he is shut in upon himself. Art will never succeed in concealing the fact that this muttering, this enormous rumbling which opens the drunkard's reverie in *Finnegans Wake*, is a caricature, a sort of inversion of the creative and revealing "Word" which resounds through the opening of Genesis and St. John's Gospel.[37]

In the same way the Greek myth of Alcestis and the Christian hope of salvation are both woven into the thread of T. S. Eliot's *Cocktail Party*. There where "gossip" painfully hides the emptiness of existence, Eliot unveils a fundamental human failure: Edward and Lavinia are shadows in

[37]Cf. C. Moeller, "The Image of Man in Modern European Literature," *Student World* (1962), 153–54, 155, 156, 157.

search of reality. Likewise, in *The Elder Statesman*, Lord Claverton is a type of Oedipus to Colonus. In the recognition of his failure as a father, one gets a glimpse of the existence of a deeper paternity, a religious meaning to his apparently empty existence, and his daughter, an Antigone to this aged Oedipus, illuminates this destiny with a shaft of filial love, which suggests a religious dimension.[38] Such a reading of the meaning of man's image is possible only in the light of religion. Joyce's Catholic background and Eliot's Anglicanism are the proof of this. But even with non-believers like William Faulkner the very force of what he had to say about man made him take a series of biblical expressions borrowed from Creation and the Fall; only this vocabulary could express what Faulkner deeply felt, for example, in *Requiem for a Nun*. The same is true of Penn-Warren and many others.

The profane exegesis of the texts cited remains valid. But a more profound exegesis offers us a final complement, revealing there the hand of God. Even those who do not believe can be interested in the light which this hypothesis throws on reality. God is revealed as hidden in the fibre of this image of man, and as the Father who incarnates the law which, enumerating good and evil, restores life.

So true it is that all knowledge of nothingness and of sin is not good. It is God who judges; in the last analysis it is He alone, in the revelation of His Word, who accuses, challenges, judges and saves. Only thus can man have, in his condition as a sinner before God, the kind of knowledge which is also conversion.

There is thus in the secular literature of the present century planetary hope and cosmic fear, appeals from God and appeals to God, but buried in the sand like footprints on the sea-shore whose meaning is lost.[39]

[38]C. du Bos, *What is Literature?* (London, 1940), p. 14ff., analyzes the literature in this sense; cf. De Raeymaeker *et al.*, *Truth and Freedom*, 116, 119–27, analysis of the literary critique.
[39]Moeller, *Student World*, 158.

Taking inspiration from the third question posed by President Murray Ross, I would like to speak finally about religious life on the university campus. It is extremely difficult to do more than offer suggestions, because the situation varies so much from university to university.

(1) If it is necessary to organize in some way the practice of religion in the university, it seems useful to show clearly that this service is *distinct* from the strictly academic administration.

(2) Seeing that, from the viewpoint of religious life on the campus, it can no longer be a question of religion or Christianity in general, it seems desirable, if a place of worship is set aside for the practice of religion, to have it open to all denominations, at least all the Christian denominations. If I am not mistaken, such is the solution found at Harvard and also at the Oecumenical Institute of Heidelberg University.

(3) Concerning Christianity, the oecumenical spirit must penetrate all religious life at the university. It is not a question here of relativism or "debased irenicism" but of mutual knowledge and profound respect, as well as concrete social collaboration in a series of activities of the type of "*Life and Work*," I am thinking, for example, of what Christians can contribute to solving problems such as racial segregation and the status of women in different societies. It is not a question of following a fashion but, on the contrary, of searching for a deeper truth.

(4) It seems even more necessary to safeguard liberty from all constraint. Liberty in adhering to a religion is a human value in itself; at the same time, it affirms a theological fact, that the believer in the act of faith is obeying the voice of God. We must avoid all proselytism, that is, all action aimed at introducing into religious life any social,

economic, or cultural constraint or any form of pressure. This, of course, does not take away the possibility and even the usefulness of bearing witness to religious faith, but on a purely religious level. Between the cacophony of the "fairground of ideas," the "universal exposition of thought" before which the European intellectual hesitates and dreams,[40] and the sheep-like conformity of the fanatical masses, there is the positive reality of religious conviction, based on religious motives. In the pluralist society to which we belong, it would be unreal and false to promote a religious unity which would be a uniformity imposed by social pressure.

These principles, worked out in collaboration by theologians of the World Council of Churches and the Catholic Conference for Oecumenical Questions, must find a place in every university. We dare to hope, moreover, that the Second Vatican Council, by its statement on religious liberty, will make delicate but quite clear statements on these points. The address of the Bishop of Bruges in presenting this decree allows us to make such a forecast.[41]

(5) Up until the present time, the religious faith of the majority of believers has been supported by the social and cultural order of the milieu. Now for the first time in humanity's religious history a growing number of the faithful must live their faith without the help of this sociological environment. Society is becoming secularized, "se laïcise" in French. What was, up until the present, the vocation of a few individuals of exceptionally strong character has now become the common lot. The decline in the practice of religion throughout the world can be explained, in part, by this fact.

This disappearance of sociological supports, the more

[40]P. Valéry, "La Crise de l'esprit," *in Œuvres complètes*, vol. I (ed. *La pléiade*, Paris, 1957), pp. 993–94.
[41]French text of this speech by Mgr. de Smedt in *Documentation catholique*, no. 1415 (January 5, 1964), cols. 71–81.

and more obvious impossibility of limiting ourselves to being "fairy-tale" Christians, can be the occasion of a deepening of religious life, in the sense of a conscious and voluntary approach; more than fifty years ago Père de Grandmaison called it "personal religion." Religious life on the campus must take this personal step and it can do so, for between the almost eremitical solitude, which is the vocation of several outstanding individuals such as Charles de Foucauld, and the conformity to a religion which is more sociological than religious there is the living proof of small groups, which are called in France "équipes religieuses."

What are small groups? Up to about thirty members, for beyond that, according to Aldous Huxley's fine remark, there is the crowd with its own psychology. The important thing is not so much the number but the spirit of dialogue with the university environment. Dialogue does not mean eclecticism, relativism, the absence of self-affirmation, but only an "openness." Charles de Foucauld, living in his "open hermitage," received all those who came to speak with him, about religion or any other subject; thus he became a "brother to all men." On the contrary, the student Joseph D., in Julian Green's novel *Moïra*, is undoubtedly a believer burning with love of God, with the desire for complete purity, but he is alone, deprived of all contact with a small group where his faith would be stabilized and deepened; he has no intercourse with others. It is only necessary to remember the scene in his room when he hears, through a very thin partition wall, what others are saying about women and love; he stays, transfixed with horror, and soon he is fascinated.

This universal openness is a question of life or death. If not in a university, where honesty in research and exchange must be presented to permit frank discussion on these questions, then I do not know where it can be found. Unfortunately, religious groups all have a tendency to hide themselves under a sort of protective shell; they develop a special form of deafness to "those who do not think as we do." A publicist recently said that it is the good misfortune of the Roman cardinals never to catch morning trains! The ship, the Church, cannot stay in a dry-dock; the so-called eleventh commandment: "Thou shalt not rock the boat" is an invention of those who wish to safeguard the purity of the pearl of faith without ever taking it from its jewel-case. Too often, religious language is jargon, when it is not a "Canaanite dialect" unintelligible to those who are not of the faith and even to those who are, as a Bishop said rather amusingly at the council. "We must make sure that the life of the Church has a new way of feeling, of willing and of bearing itself," said Paul VI at Bethlehem. Here he seems to express one of the major intentions of the council. Its realization is urgent because far too many people identify Christianity with a negative morality. For many, the Catholic is the person who does not divorce and who has a lot of children. Certainly divorce is forbidden by the Church, and children express the profound meaning of marriage, although marriage is even more an image, distant but real, of the union of Christ and the Church. But where is the proof of this in the world? How many know that Christianity is communion, life, resurrection? How many people understood at first sight what Archbishop Ramsey said in his admirable book, *The Resurrection of Christ*: "For the first disciples of the Gospel without the Resurrection was not merely a Gospel without its final chapter: *it was not a Gospel at all.*"[42]

(6) I do not know what the situation is in the other Christian denominations. In current Catholic theology there is too great a tendency to identify the Church with a clerical pyramid, with the Pope at the top, then the bishops, too often confused with the Pope's "messenger boys," then the

[42]A. M. Ramsey, *The Resurrection of Christ* (London, 1961), p. 9.

priests, and, *last but least*, the pious laity, the "choir boys" or, as Père Congar said, the "clientele." Edouard le Roy had already said many years ago that in the Church the laity were like the sheep at Candlemas whom one sheared and blessed. It was more than funny when Cardinal Gasquet once stated that the laity in the Church have two positions: sitting up to hear the sermon and kneeling down to receive the blessing—to which a mischievous Irish priest added a third, that of the layman with his hand on his wallet to put money in the collection! We have passed by the question which Archbishop Ullathorne put to John Henry Newman, asking why he spoke so much about laymen and finally wanting to know what indeed are the laity. To this Newman replied: "I do not know, but I think the Church would look rather foolish without them!"

We must avoid all clericalism. A Christian civilization is not necessarily an ecclesiastical one, even less is it a clerical one. There is too great a tendency to forget this in some Catholic ecclesiastical circles, in certain European countries at least. If we wish to offer the opportunity of living religion on the university campus, a great initiative must be left to the students themselves. I was happy to read Daniel Callahan's book, *The Mind of the Catholic Layman*, because I feel there is a new spirit in the air in its historical viewpoint of the Catholic laity as well as in the principles, stated therein.[43]

43D. Callahan, *The Mind of the Catholic Layman* (New York, 1963). See also G. Chamberlin, *Church and the Campus* (Westminster Press, 1962). A quotation from a criticism in *Weekly America*, January 18, 1964, pp. 104–5 is likewise of interest: "Churchmen, with due exception, have little understanding of the members of academic community, or sympathy for them. The churches are interested in having them as parishioners and in utilizing their services when offered, but then to disregard the fact that they have special needs in their chosen vocation, needs that these same churches could help meet. We might add that the campus area is no place for a sacristy priest. At least, one significant point emerges. While educators have a firm grasp on intermediate goals, they have little or no appreciation of ultimate values or concerns. On

The second session of the Vatican Council has underlined the irreplaceable role of the Christian layman in the church as well as in the world.[44] By his position in society he can be the living proof of religious hope in the ultimate sense of the human history of which I have spoken. The final religious orientation does not destroy the significance of this history; it does not make it the pastime of children waiting for God to drop a ready-made heaven from the sky! The desert fathers, in between their prayers, wove matting, which they would undo the next day to weave again the day after that. I do not know if this is true for we cannot trust hagiographers! But today, when clothing and shelter are far too scarce, earthly work has a different significance to that given it by the venerable fathers of the desert!

The world is divided between fear and hope.[45] In the small world of a university the Christian laity bear witness. If they know the essence of faith, and do not confuse it with peripheral devotions, if they are capable of attaining this "second naivety," this faith strengthened by the passage through the crucible of criticism, if they are truly open to dialogue with all students, forcing themselves to think with and in front of them the concrete problems of this world of 1964, they will avoid irritating and useless proselytism, as well as detachment; they will be witnesses, like a people dispersed in a divided world.

These groups exist. One need only think of the lay confraternities of Charles de Foucauld, of the Pauline groups, social groups, and the orthodox movement (Z01) (life)

---

the other hand, churchmen, who deal with religious ultimates, fail to give proper valuation to the intermediate goals, with which most members of the faculty and the student body must involve themselves. The writer emphasizes the need for the church to put off anti-intellectualism. The church must accept the university colleges as they are. It is a secular field of research."

[44]A colloquy was organized in Glion by the Copecial and the Dea on the laity, at the end of January.

[45]Cf. Mende, *Entre la peur et l'espoir.*

which is attempting a renewal of religious life in the secularized regions of Greek life. These scattered people act
like a leaven. May they appear as witnesses of the transcendence of the hidden God and of the light which religion
brings to the semi-darkness of all life, as well as to the wonderful efforts of human endeavour in the search for justice
and love.

IV

These are the thoughts I give you on the questions posed by
the President of this university. I have not spoken of
Catholicism in the university, but I have outlined the possible attitude of a Catholic faced with this problem. I would
rather say of a Christian, if I have succeeded in speaking in
an oecumenical spirit.

The seriousness of the question posed in this series of
"lectures," as well as the marked humanist sympathies
shown by York University, are a great joy to me. I will conclude by quoting the words of a man who loved the New
World, where he was received so kindly in 1919 after
World War I, Cardinal Mercier. The founder of the Institut
Supérieur de Philosophie at Louvain University, he was also
the soul of the Malines Conversations, a landmark in the
history of oecumenism. In a report in 1901 he said:

The profession of Christian faith must not be an obstacle to the
generous initiatives of the scholar or even the daring procedures
of the genius. The Church has never held it to be her mission to
cut down errors as soon as they make their appearance. She
often knows how to wait and let an error succumb under the
weight of its own consequences, for she is convinced that error
can be the forerunner of truth and frequently its companion.
She knows that to wrest a particle of truth from the unknown,
man's mind must often travel over long and arduous paths in
which, at first sight, he may seem to get lost.[46]

46De Raeymaeker *et al., Truth and Freedom,* p. 16.

But, at the same time as he affirmed this genuine acceptance of scientific advances, he underlined, in an address at the university on December 8, 1907, the importance of the humanist approach in conjunction with the religious approach:

Man is not a pure intellect which, within the enclosure of a laboratory abstracts a formal object. Outside the hours reserved for the soaring flights of the mind, there is also a time for the harmonious development of all the faculties of a human being and for those loftier powers of the Christian soul.[47]

[47]*Ibid.*, p. 17.

The Relationship between Religion and the Educational Function of the University

Alexander Wittenberg

Alexander Wittenberg

Alexander Wittenberg is Professor of Mathematics, York University, Toronto, Canada. Dr. Wittenberg studied mathematics, physics, and philosophy at the Eidgenössische Technische Hochschule in Zürich, Switzerland, receiving his doctorate of mathematics in 1955. After several teaching appointments in Europe, he taught mathematics at Laval University, Quebec, where he also did research in philosophy and pedagogy. Dr. Wittenberg is the author of Bildung und Mathematik: Mathematik als exemplarisches Gymnasialfach *and* Vom Denken in Begriffen.

WHEN a new university such as York asks about the relationship between religion and the university, we may take for granted that it wants, and is entitled to, practical answers. When it asks this question of men who have devoted their lives to the supremely practical task of learning, thinking, and teaching others to learn and to think, we know that it is aware that the truly practical answers are those that bridge the gap between principle and action, rescuing the principle from the sterility of a purely academic exercise, and the action from the ever renewed foolishness of mere expediency.

It is by no means a matter of course that this kind of question should be asked on such terms. The very fact illuminates both the frame of reference in which we should seek an answer to the question, and the nature of the university that is asking it. Like some men, some universities are becoming increasingly other-directed, to adopt David Riesman's already classic phrase. To them, their duty is to do whatever others expect them to do, whether it makes sense or not—to satisfy a "public demand for university education" in the same sense in which other establishments satisfy a public demand for Coca Cola or "rock 'n roll" records, and with the same sort of business acumen. In such a context, the question about religion and the university will be asked of market analysts and specialists in public relations, ultimately to be decided by so-called "men of action" whose claim to that title is that they clearly are not men of ideas, and are free from all the inhibitions, restraints, and ideals that awareness of great and long-range tasks brings to the solution of little and short-range problems.

York University was born with a higher and prouder sense of purpose. The early book[1] by its President, Murray G. Ross, was a manifesto of inner-directedness, a manifesto of the will of this university to seek its own understanding

[1]*The New University* (Toronto, 1961).

of its duty, to seek it in penetrating insights into the contemporary needs of society, and also to abide by it. The book also was a manifesto of the will to teach such insights to those who might need to learn, as indeed is the function of a true university. It would truly be ironical if an institution devoted to the attainment and spreading of knowledge failed in attaining and spreading knowledge of its own true function!

This proud and responsible understanding of the task confronting a new university dictates the terms on which we should deal with our topic today. The demand upon us clearly is to examine the relationship between religion and the university within the basic terms of reference of what a university has to be, and in such a way as to arrive at a concrete interpretation of the duty of a university in this particular area. This, then, is the challenge that I have in mind in presenting the following observations to you.[2] Because the subject is vast, and my time quite limited, I shall focus my remarks on that part of the problem which seems to me to be the most important: the relationship between religion and the educational task of the university. But I shall start by stating my views on a number of other aspects of the problem, without, however, elaborating on them.

First of all, religion is a legitimate and, indeed, a privileged private concern of the individual. It has, therefore, a legitimate and worthwhile role to play in the extracurricular life on the university campus. Moreover, it is the duty of the university to safeguard the private religious convictions of its members to the full extent that this is possible without infringing upon more essential duties. To give an example: in my view, the university may *not* compel an orthodox

2These observations are an expanded version of a brief talk that the author gave to a student-faculty symposium at York University, shortly after the close of the public lecture series on "Religion and the University." The views expressed are his own.

Jew to write an examination on the Sabbath. It *may*, however, compel him to take lectures in which religions, including his own, are examined from an objective standpoint— for instance the standpoint of a comparative study of religions, or that of sociology. Furthermore, I do not believe that the university should establish for that student an orthodox Jewish residence, which would shield its members from intellectual contact and debate with members of other faiths. And what I have just said applies equally, of course, to the Roman Catholic, the Anglican, or, for that matter, the militant atheist.

On the other hand, religious observances of any kind have no business whatsoever in the official and ceremonial life of the university. This principle is a direct consequence of the basic commitment of the university (to which I shall return in a moment). The university is dedicated to the pursuit of truth, wherever this may lead. It may lead some of its members to the view that religion is a gift from God, and others to the view that it is opium for the people. The university as an institution dare not take sides between them, not even by intimation. The only thing that it should intimate to all its members, and particularly to its students, is a passionate dedication to truthfulness. This dedication is clearly violated when the university as a corporate body performs religious exercises which are potentially meaningless or worse to some of those who make up the university. I might add that this matter is of particular significance in a new university. In very old institutions, the patina of the centuries sometimes endows traditional ceremonies with a meaning of their own which is different from their manifest meaning. (The reluctance to assume office traditionally exhibited by a newly appointed speaker to the House of Commons no longer has the meaning of an expression of genuine fear. It is meaningful nevertheless.) In new institutions, such ceremonials appear naked, carrying no other meaning than the obvious and superficial one. Thus religious observances in universities entail either an intolerable violation of the basic commitment of the university, or intolerable hypocrisy, or an intolerable exhibition of what is understood by all concerned to be but a meaningless comedy.[3]

As far as research is concerned, I entirely agree with Professor Pelikan's stand that theological research is an important intellectual concern of man. It therefore has a legitimate and worthwhile place among the scholarly research on the university campus, and the university will be the richer for sharing in this kind of endeavour. To be sure, theological research can be of widely varying quality. The university would hardly benefit if it were to harbour narrow-minded "research" about some obscure details of theology, research which would cut itself off deliberately from, and contribute nothing to, its over-all intellectual life. But the same obviously is true of every other field of knowledge as well.

All these, however, are relatively minor issues. Our central problem, as I said, is that of the relationship between religion and the educational function of the university. In saying this, I am making the tacit assumption that the university *does* have an educational function to perform, and that this, indeed, is an essential part of its mission. This remark may appear trivial, but only because the word "education" is becoming increasingly ambiguous. It is unnecessary to add that the university has to "educate" specialists in computer technology and mediaeval church history, and that it has to be a repository of specialized knowledge about these and similarly remote fields. The

    [3]It is in no way improper, of course, for those members of a university who are faithful believers to pray for divine guidance and protection at solemn moments of the academic year. But they can do this either in separate religious services before or after official ceremonies, or during these very ceremonies in moments of silent meditation.

educational function to which I was referring extends far beyond this. It is to produce successive generations of educated men and women, in the old sense of the word "educated" that does not require further qualification; and it also is to be within society an ever-flowing source of creative concern for the basic and central problems of man. This is the frame of reference in which I propose to discuss our topic now.[4]

Religious experience in its many forms has been, and still is, one of the deepest spiritual experiences of man. It is, therefore, not only legitimate, but indeed essential that students should acquire an understanding of this experience in some of its greatest manifestations. (This is in keeping with the more basic principle that the teaching of a university, and particularly its general education programme, should focus on the truly central concerns of man. Students are entitled to expect that we shall not take up their time with trivia, but shall meet head-on the most significant aspects of the human condition, those that are of greatest potential concern to a thoughtful man.)

Now, as several speakers in our lecture series have pointed out, religious experience (for instance what Professor Moeller called the experience of the holy) can be had only from the inside, as it were. We do not understand it if we know only *of it* or *about it*. There is therefore only one way to convey understanding of it: it is to convey a measure of empathy for it. We have to come to understand through

[4]The primary (but by no means the only) focus of this kind of educational concern within the university will be its general educational programme and herein in particular lies the seminal importance of the latter. I have amplified this aspect in my inaugural lecture at York University, "General Education as a Challenge for Creative Scholarship," publication forthcoming by York University.

"Religion" might well be made the theme for a whole general education course, in the sense of the "thematic approach" described in this lecture. The remarks made below may then be taken as an outline of the possible content of such a course.

empathy what it is for a man truly to live in a religious faith—even, and particularly, a faith we ourselves do not share. We must come to respect an alien faith, not with the shallow tolerance which we have for our brother's idiosyncrasies, his likes and dislikes of things such as curling or fish soup, but rather with that deep tolerance which is but a reflection of a deeply rooted awareness that our own experience, insight, or wisdom is not the whole of experience, insight, or wisdom.

It will be clear that in making these remarks I am thinking very much in educational terms. The primary reason for conveying this kind of understanding to a student is not that we thereby further desirable social aims like tolerance and social peace, although this, of course, is an important side effect. Our primary aim is to enrich the individual student's own inner experience and his vision of life, and at the same time to broaden and deepen his capacity for empathy for his fellow man. Bigotry always is foolishness even before it is a threat to society. And the whole function of a university is to fight against the foolishness of man.

This thought, of course, brings up the question of whether it is possible to acquire empathy for a religious faith that we do not share? I believe that it is.[5] The method is clear. Such empathy is acquired by meeting, with wide-awake sensitivity, great minds who are deeply imbued with that faith. There are many possibilities for this. To quote one less obvious example, I believe that a musically sensitive person can learn to understand something of what the resurrection of Christ is to a faithful Christian by hearing

[5]In making this statement, I think back with gratitude to Henri Agel, a brilliant and devout Catholic, the teacher who "taught" me during the fruitful and stimulating years that I spent as a student in France's outstanding and most secular schools. By teaching me a measure of empathy and understanding for his faith, on the firm basis of fairness and open-mindedness of the French school system, he contributed immeasurably to what American educationists would call my "intellectual growth."

the extraordinary transition from the Crucifixion to the Resurrection in J. S. Bach's B Minor Mass.

I stated above that religious experience is one of the great spiritual experiences of mankind. But there are many essentially different kinds of religious experiences. And this fact also is one of the deep spiritual experiences of man. It is not enough for a student to acquire empathy and understanding for one kind of religious experience, one faith, only. If his own spiritual experience remains thus limited, he is in fact being misled. He must rather come to integrate within his own experience the reality of the existence of a plurality of faiths. To that end the university should convey to its students a measure of genuine empathy for at least two radically different religious faiths, taking these up in their most significant and valuable features, and *in what makes them different*. This argument militates against a vague and loosely conceived "oecumenical" approach. The focus must lie, not in the vague generalities that the religions have in common, but in the deep spiritual experiences that give them their peculiar individuality and differentiate them from each other. A particularly striking example is provided by the contrast between the emphasis of all our Western religions on monotheism and those Eastern religious experiences for whom the jealous emphasis on exclusiveness inherent in monotheism is something barbaric.

There is a third deep existential experience which belongs to the general context of religious experience, and which must also be understood through empathy. This is the experience of the rejection of religion—of a human existence in which there is no room for a religious faith. I am thinking not so much of the atheist as of the agnostic experience. This, I believe, represents an unprecedented combination of existential humility and boldness—accepting to live an existential commitment without the support and reassurance of a faith. It is an experience which, explicitly, and even more implicitly, is very typical of our modern world. It has two facets: on the one hand, the experience that much is required of us while little guarantees are granted us in our life, and, on the other hand, the experience that we are "dust and shall return to dust" and yet make bold to affirm and uphold *our* standards and values to the universe.[6]

All that I have said so far could be summed up in the statement that it is part of education to acquire through empathy an understanding for living *with* a faith, for living with a *different* faith, and for living *without* a faith.

But religion[7] is not understood through empathy alone. Nor is religious experience all there is to religion. We have learned also to understand religion as a social, an intellectual, a psychological, a historical, and an economic phenomenon. And this type of understanding, which views religion as an objective phenomenon to be studied, not as an experience to be shared, is complementary to the former one, in the strict philosophical meaning of the word "complementary." It is this kind of understanding that the social historian, the specialist in the comparative study of religions, the economist who is concerned with the interrelationship between the economic structure of a society and its religious beliefs, all seek to attain. It is essential for the education of our students that they be exposed to this way of looking at religion as well. We do not understand the religious experience if we have never viewed it otherwise than with detachment—but neither do we understand it if we have failed to view it with detachment too.

---

[6]There is almost a premonition of this in one of the most extraordinary passages of the Bible—Abraham's haggling with God over Sodom and Gomorrha, when he makes bold to admonish his Maker (Genesis xviii. 25): "Far be it from Thee to do such a thing, to slay the righteous with the wicked, so that the righteous fare as the wicked! Far be that from Thee! Shall not the judge of all the earth do right?"

[7]In the following discussion, "religious experience" and "religion" should be understood to include the agnostic experience, agnosticism, and atheism.

This detached view must include (and this often is neglected) a balanced and sober survey of what religion is in practical reality—in the actual beliefs of those who are said to share it, in the sermons of its priests, in the books by which it teaches its young or its future ministers. The parish bulletin is a religious document too, and in many respects a most significant one!

At the beginning of these remarks, I stated that it was our duty to seek to answer the question before us in concrete terms, that is, so as to provide guidelines for practical action. Do the ideas outlined so far fit that requirement? It is obvious that there are many institutions calling themselves "universities" for which the above suggestions would be utterly impractical, if not downright fantastic. This is because implicit in these ideas is a well defined conception of the sort of environment that a true university should provide for its members, both teachers and students, and, indeed, of the nature of a true university.

A university should be a place in which the very air one breathes is permeated with passionate, creative, open-minded concern for basic problems and great issues confronting man. This is much more than just saying that a university should be a place of scholarship and research. It means that this research and scholarship should be the outgrowth and expression of a passionate commitment to the attainment of knowledge worth having. And, more than anything else, it is this passionate commitment that a student should meet and acquire in a university. He should learn from Plato what it is to strive after truth and virtue (and not just how to write commentaries on Plato's commentators). He should learn from Einstein the longing for the understanding of nature in simple mathematical terms (and not just that $E = mc^2$).

Yet it is not enough to speak of passionate commitment. This may actually be misleading. After all, nowhere is passionate commitment to great and basic issues confronting man more alive than in a great monastery. Yet a monastery is not a university. The peculiar quality of the university environment derives from the distinctive nature of the commitment which lives in it. It is a commitment that incorporates a deep intellectual and existential humility, an all-pervading acknowledgment both that the genuine search for truth includes a constant search for challenges to whatever an individual holds true and that there are more aspects to truth and more ways of searching for it than any one individual is able to incorporate into his own personal experience at any one time. A monastery would cease to be that if it tried to harbour two different and contradictory basic truths at the same time, or kept eagerly looking for challenges to its truths. A university begins to be a university only when it does precisely that. This is why I spoke a moment ago of the "open-minded concern" which must be alive in a university.

In brief, the university environment derives its peculiar quality from the way in which it integrates passionate commitment with intellectual open-mindedness and catholicity. In our day and age, it is important to note that it really takes both elements to constitute the spirit of a true university. Clearly, an institution is not a university in this sense if it submits, explicitly or tacitly, to the *a priori* dictate of dogma, be it theological or ideological dogma, or even the dogma of "public opinion." But neither is it a university if it lacks the passion altogether, if its open-mindedness is not fed by important concerns, and if it wants to be no more than a place where, as the saying goes, the "bland lead the bland"—to a degree.

To revert now to our theme, religion and the university, it is clear that the stand that I took above not only is appropriate to this kind of environment, but is, in fact, dictated by it. All I really did was to spell out this general view of the nature of a true university environment in terms of the specific problem that was before us.

It should be spelled out a little further. I said a moment ago that I agreed with Professor Pelikan's remarks concerning the relevance of theological research to a university. It will be seen now that much more than just straightforward research within the several particular theological frameworks can and should take place within the university. The university should be the privileged setting for a continuous intellectual confrontation between the various faiths, as well as between faith as such and the agnostic experience on the one hand, the objective sociological one on the other. Such a confrontation should be marked by the classical features of university debate on any subject: fairness and tolerance combined with intellectual rigour and fed by a genuine desire on the part of the participants to learn from each other. It should be a dialogue between men accepting and respecting each other in their differences for the sake of a common pursuit of truth.

Let me take this opportunity to state two great tasks which, I believe, loom ahead waiting to be tackled by the universities in such a spirit. One is the task of attacking on its merits, and independently from a theological framework, the great old question of good and evil, and of our knowledge of good and evil, attacking it, to be sure, not as a topic for abstruse philosophical speculation, but as a living intellectual issue which lies at the very heart of our social, individual, and also intellectual life. And the other task is that of taking a long hard look at religion in the light of such an inquiry, the task, in other words, of explicitly asking the question of the relationship between religion and morality—a question in comparison with which the old and worn out question of the relationship between religion and science pales into insignificance.

But we must widen our perspective still further. I have

been discussing what a university environment should be. But an environment is related to what should take place in the environment as the organ is related to the function. What is the basic function of the university?

A university has many functions, of course. They range from the education of learned specialists needed by society to the maintenance of a haven of intellectual rationality within society. But I believe that all these functions derive from a more basic one. This is to keep vigorously alive a most peculiar kind of intellectual commitment—a commitment of which we have only begun to discover the power and originality during the last few centuries. Superficially, the commitment is a very old one. It is the commitment to the search for important truths. What is new is our understanding of what it means, and of the intellectual demands that it places upon us. This new understanding is, I believe, one of the greatest conquests of modern man.

The originality of our modern conception of the search for truth lies in the fact that in integrates two seemingly contradictory aspects. On the one hand, it commits us to a passionate pursuit of particular lines of inquiry, with intellectual means of ever increasing rigour and power. Yet at the same time it also commits us to a basic intellectual humility, to an acknowledgement of the legitimacy, not only of questions that have not yet been asked and might be inconceivable for us today, but also of questions that are essentially different from, and possibly diametrically opposite to, the various questions that we are investigating in our own inquiries. This implies much more than just the shallow tolerance which would allow for peaceful coexistence of mutually incompatible pursuits ignoring each other. What really is implied is the strong positive tolerance which affirms that all these pursuits are essential, that it is only the whole of them that makes up the pursuit of truth, and also that every single inquiry must constantly face up to the challenge of all the others.[8] As this commitment was increasingly understood and upheld, it led to an enormous widening of our experience of what the search for truth encompasses; and this widening experience, which today includes areas of intellectual endeavour that are as different as psychoanalysis or the sociology of knowledge is from mathematical physics, acted as a feedback to justify the commitment and make us ever more clearly aware of its nature, value, and implications.

The function of the university, I said, is to maintain that commitment vigorously alive; the university is the organ that serves that function. In other words, the university really is the affirmation of that commitment and its translation into practical reality. Dedicated to every aspect of the search for truth, and to every one of its yet unspecified future implications, the university does not identify itself with any of them. The university is thus the very model of a free society. Also, the members of the university, to the extent that they fully and consciously are that, are the very models of citizens of a free society: men and women who are steeped in particular pursuits and convictions, yet aware that these are but a part of a whole to which conflicting pursuits and convictions do belong; men and women who are able to reconcile within themselves deep involvement in their own and personal knowledge with a measure of detachment from it and with an awareness, not only that their

[8]It may be noted that the commitment described above is, at the same time, an epistemological commitment relating to the nature of our knowledge, and a moral commitment relating to a moral duty. A most forceful and penetrating analysis of the nature of knowledge in terms that are really adequate to the modern understanding of the search for truth described above has been given by Michael Polanyi in his writings developing the idea of "personal knowledge," particularly in his book with that title (Chicago, 1958). As to the epistemological status of truth on these terms, it has, in effect, been discussed to some extent in my book *Vom Denken in Begriffen* (Birkhäuser, Basel, 1958).

own knowledge is limited, but also that it is bound to limitations and open to challenges of which they are not aware.

In the last analysis, it is clear that this kind of commitment cannot coexist on a par with a religious commitment. It must either claim precedence over the latter, or submit to its pre-eminence. A religious faith is exclusive by its very nature. A university that would be exclusive is not a university. There cannot be a monastery serving two different gods at once. There cannot be a university dedicated to the service of only one god. There is an inherent conflict between the absolute commitment to one particular truth that is held revealed by God, and the university's open commitment, which is a commitment, not to a truth, but to a search for truth wherever the search may lead.

Let us be clear about it, this inherent conflict must be resolved in actual practice, and it can only be resolved one way or the other. One solution is to grant pre-eminence to the doctrinal framework of one particular dogma. This is what the Catholic universities do explicitly and as a matter of principle, and this is why in the deepest sense they are not, I believe, universities. The other solution is explicitly to affirm the pre-eminence of the open commitment to the search for truth, and to make acknowledgment of that pre-eminence in effect a tacit condition of citizenship in the university.

In the very last analysis, there is no escaping the conclusion that we are here faced with a genuine conflict of values. The affirmation of the university commitment, in the sense it is defined above, really is the affirmation of the moral superiority of the values embodied in it over the values of exclusiveness embodied in a religious faith. And the acknowledgment to which I was referring above, however tacit and painless it may be in actual practice, really is an acknowledgment of that superiority. It is not for me to examine how this can be mastered by the individual religious from their varies doctrinal standpoints.

Let me conclude by spelling out the implications of all this for the individual members of the university. It is clear from all I have said that the university has room for, and welcomes, many particular commitments—and this, I believe, includes the exposition of these commitments in teaching, subject naturally to normal standards of fairness and scholarship. In fact, I believe that it is vital for the university to be made up of committed individuals. The mortal danger for it are not those with strong views, but those with no views at all except on the most minor matters—the bland intellectual nonentities. The diversity of commitments is vital to the university, and so is, I might almost say, the enjoyment of the diversity by every member of the university.

It is equally vital that these commitments be freely arrived at, and freely held. They must really be the fruit of the individual's basic commitment to the search for truth. In particular, a faculty member must be accountable for his beliefs to his own conscience only, and must, therefore, be free to change them as he may find himself dictated to do so by his own pursuit of truth. In most scholarly fields, this is a matter of course. It would clearly be ridiculous for a university to appoint a scientist on the condition that he stick to some particular scientific theory. It follows from our analysis that the same freedom must be provided for faculty members in matters of faith—and this applies equally to, and in fact applies particularly to, those faculty members who were appointed to teach religious commitments. The deeper committed those whose academic duties are bound up with a faith, the greater the likelihood that some among them will experience profound shifts in religious experience —that there will be a Luther or a Pascal among them. A university environment must leave them as free for this change as it leaves the scientist free to shift his allegiance from one scientific theory to another.

Finally, the student in a university is entitled to *respect* for his faith—he is not entitled to *protection* for it. As a member of the university, he is committed to share in the over-all commitment of his alma mater. He cannot refuse the involvement in the whole range of the search for truth. He may not, in particular, reject the confrontation with other kinds of faith, with the absence of faith, or with the objective study of the phenomenon of faith. Does this mean that he must accept the destruction of his own personal faith? By no means! Or rather, only to the extent that exposure to such experiences is enough to effect the destruction. In fact, such an education may result for some actually in the loss of their faith, for others in the transformation of their faith from a childish into a mature and deeply rooted one. What matters is that it should generally result in refining shallow and superficial commitments into deep and mature ones.

The university's concern is to graduate its students as mature and truly educated adults. It is in the nature of things that the commitments of these adults will reflect the whole range of commitments to which the search for truth leads man. By that very fact, they will carry over into society at large some of the ethos of the university. What greater compliment could be paid a university than if it could truly be said of it that it is a nursery of a free society?

Date Due

JE 4 '65		
MY - 4 '66		
AG 4 '69		
AP 24 '72		
AP 24 '72		
JAN 16 '79		
APR 16 '79		
	—	